CASEFILES

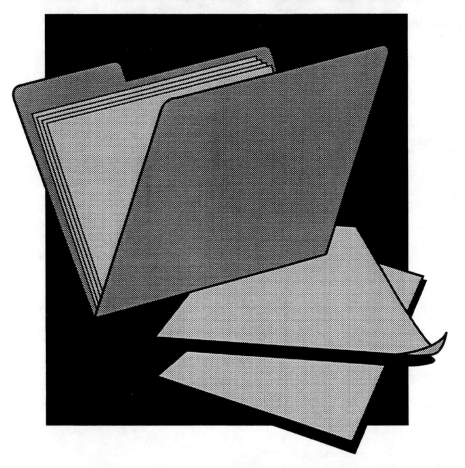

Instructor's Supplement

Linda J. Carpenter, Ph.D.
Department of Communication Disorders
University of Wisconsin-Eau Claire

Thinking Publications
Eau Claire, WI

ISBN 0-930599-38-1

**THINKING
PUBLICATIONS®**
A Division of McKinley Companies, Inc.

424 Galloway Street
Eau Claire, WI 54703

(715) 832-2488
FAX (715) 832-9082

Table of Contents

Introduction to CaseFiles Instructor's Supplement

The *CaseFiles* textbook, *CaseFiles* Appraisal Plan poster, and accompanying computer program were created as a teaching tool to help faculty facilitate students' clinical problem-solving skills in assessment of children and adolescents with suspected communication disorders. The purposes of these introductory comments are to describe the contents of the *Instructor's Supplement,* to provide tips for using case method teaching, to describe the author's use of cases in instruction, to highlight features of the *CaseFiles* computer program, and to provide an overview of the cases included in the computer program. The *Instructor's Supplement* is sufficiently detailed so that faculty can feel comfortable with each case's planning and outcomes, without investing hours of time on the computer simulation tasks.

CONTENTS OF THE INSTRUCTOR'S SUPPLEMENT

The *Instructor's Supplement* is provided as an aid for faculty in using *CaseFiles* with their students. It includes several sets of information:

- A summary of relevant background information for each case is provided so that faculty can become familiar with historical data without having to work through the Interview Outcomes section of the computer program. This background statement also synthesizes the medical and educational information that is presented in depth in the *CaseFiles* text.

- Appraisal Outcome data for each case are provided so that faculty will have "answers" available without having to score and interpret performances themselves. Under the child-based domain, standardized test data include raw scores, standard scores, standard error of measurement values, and percentile ranks as well as age equivalents when appropriate. For informal procedures, descriptions of performances are provided. In addition, interpretive statements are given for the various areas of performance included in the appraisal under the child-based domain. Appraisal outcomes under the setting-based domain are also summarized and interpreted.

- Suggested questions for class discussion are provided to help faculty facilitate students' critical thinking in planning assessments and interpreting assessment data. Careful questioning stands at the center of case method teaching, and it is assumed that instructors will develop their own questions to guide discussion about issues in assessment that are reflected in the cases of *CaseFiles*. However, the questions raised in this *Instructor's Guide* are suggested because the author has found them useful in facilitating discussion and critical consideration of salient issues. Each question is followed by a brief discussion that highlights some relevant points.

Some of the suggested discussion questions are linked directly to the assessment-intervention process. For example, questions such as, "Does this child demonstrate a language disorder?" and "What predictions can be made about this child's future language learning and use?" address the assessment-intervention phases of diagnosis and prognosis, respectively, and they are raised for each case. While clearly related to the basic questioning inherent in assessment planning and interpretation of outcomes, these questions will likely be addressed in different ways for each of the cases. Such variations in response considerations offer rich opportunities for addressing language theory issues and their relationship to practice.

Other questions reflect an intent to debrief with students about their problem solving and decision-making. For example, a question such as, "What differences are noted in student and actual appraisal plans?" is posed to help students think critically about the choices they have made in planning. Discussion of this kind of question will contribute to students' realization that there are rarely "right" answers in assessment planning and that different plan strategies may well lead to similar conclusions about a child. The opportunities for facilitating critical thinking and for linking theory to practice seem clear.

Other types of questions focus on critical thinking with respect to use of normative data and different appraisal methods. Questions such as, "What is the relative utility of qualitative versus quantitative methods with this child?" encourage students to think about appraisal methodology and the kinds of strategies selected to meet plan specifications. Again, the opportunities for linking theory and practice are rich.

Still other suggested discussion questions specifically address theories and their relationship to practice. Questions such as, "What is the relationship between oral and written language?" and "What is the relationship between language and cognition?" clearly address issues in language theories. Raising these questions in class discussion provides students with opportunities to think critically about observed language performances and how they relate to various theoretical paradigms. While these theory-to- practice questions could easily be addressed for each case, they are more salient with some of the cases than with others. Thus, the same theory-driven questions are not necessarily posed for each case in *CaseFiles*.

Another type of suggested discussion question is case specific. These questions tend to focus on ideas that will help students gain and use substantive information relevant to particular cases. Questions such as, "What is the effect of Ritalin and other stimulant drugs on children's behaviors?" and "What skills and attitudes are involved in using interpreters in assessment?" do not apply to all of the children represented in *CaseFiles*. Yet for relevant cases, these questions are essential to helping students problem solve effectively, and the opportunities for rich discussion are clear.

One question in particular is relevant to all of the cases in *CaseFiles,* and it deserves special attention here. The question is not presented as a formal discussion point but is likely to be asked by students. Specifically, "Why do most of the decision trees look so sparse?" Visual inspection of the decision tree developed for each case shows that the tree looks relatively barren, with only a few branches completed. This observation may be problematic for some students, but it provides the opportunity to address the notion of sampling throughout the appraisal process. In that regard, the decision tree represents an ideal, but it is not feasible to appraise every branch and sub-branch. Clinicians, therefore, must be selective in the branches they choose to examine.

A noticeable simplification of the decision tree within the computer program can be found in the language component under the setting-based domain. The computer program does not give an option to plan appraisal for basic- versus transitional- versus higher-order language levels, despite the "ideal" decision tree illustrated in the *CaseFiles* Appraisal Plan poster that captures all three levels. Neither

are comprehension and production functions of language nor language areas of phonology, morphology, syntax, semantics, or pragmatics captured in the setting-based domain of the *CaseFiles* computer program. Nonetheless, faculty should encourage students to consider language levels, functions, and areas when planning direct and indirect appraisal techniques to use with parents and teachers.

For each case, discussion will help students analyze the decision tree choices they've made and the rationale that dictated their selections. Discussion will also help students examine test and task validity, particularly in light of various theoretical perspectives on language, and think critically about task analysis and selection.

Although *CaseFiles* was created as an instructional tool, its use is not intended to be prescriptive. Rather, faculty are encouraged to use the case materials in ways that fit with their teaching styles and purposes. It may be helpful, however, to know ways in which case materials can be used most effectively.

TIPS FOR USING CASE METHOD TEACHING

As a pedagogical device, case method teaching is particularly useful in helping students understand theory in terms of practice. Because cases describe real-world situations and incorporate life's complexities, case method teaching encourages students to examine their beliefs and values, analyze and reflect, and live with ambiguity (Wasserman, 1993). Recognizing the value of case method teaching, faculty in communication disorders frequently use clinical case descriptions in classroom instruction.

Case method teaching relies on discussion strategies. Consequently, both students and faculty need to prepare cases prior to class meetings. Students' preparation requirements are discussed in Chapter 1 of the *CaseFiles* student text. Attention here will focus on the instructor's preparation process for case method teaching.

In preparing for case discussions, become familiar with the case material, identify the important concepts reflected in the case, prepare a question outline that matches the case's relevant concepts, and organize the physical space so that it is facilitative of discussion (Welty, 1989). The importance of the question plan cannot be over-emphasized because it forms the foundation for the problem solving that will occur through class discussion. Because case method teaching through discussion is a student-centered activity, also be knowledgeable about your students, what they know, and how they learn. Effective use of cases demands time, and this, too, should be included in preparation for class.

During the actual class meeting, the most important behaviors of the instructor are questioning, listening, and responding (Welty, 1989). Faculty questions help students explore the facts of the case. Beyond determining factual information, questions help students use analytic skills: considering hypothetical situations, shifting perspective, identifying points of view, and applying theory are facilitated through questioning. In addition, questions focus on action: what should or could be done immediately and in the future. Finally, questions help students evaluate consequences both in short and long term.

Because students rarely answer faculty questions in expected ways, actively listen to student responses. Moreover, communicate back to the student what was heard, in terms of both the text and the subtext of the student's words. This kind of dialogue helps participants communicate what is important to them and learn from the interaction.

After the class meeting, debrief about the discussion. For the students, this typically involves tying up loose ends and bringing the discussion to a closure point. Debriefing requires determining which conceptual points were addressed well, which points were not addressed well, and which ones were missed altogether. Debriefing also involves an evaluation of which questions worked well and which ones failed. Beyond these general tips about using case method teaching, it may also be helpful to understand how cases have been used by this author in the past.

AUTHOR'S PRIOR USE OF CASES

In using cases for instruction, students were asked to form work groups, and each group was given the opportunity to choose the case that the group members were interested in working on. This logistical strategy seemed to establish an intrinsic motivation for students because they worked intensively with cases that demonstrated elements of interest to them. Student groups prepared their cases for class presentation and discussion, and three hours of class time were devoted to presentation of each case. Use of a discussion format was intended to facilitate interaction about the cases and to reduce the distance between academic and clinical teaching and learning.

In an effort to simulate real-world problem solving, students were initially given relevant referral and case history information. On the basis of that information, students designed a background investigation; in class, they presented the known history as well as an interview plan. Given the information they wanted to know, additional data were provided to them. This strategy helped students think carefully about what they wanted to know. It also helped them revise their thinking in the face of new information. Students also planned an appraisal; in class, they presented tests and procedures to be administered, described the domains and targets addressed by each test or procedure, provided a rationale for their selections, and hypothesized expected results and interpretation dimensions. In instances when standardized tests were selected, students also described technical adequacy of the instruments used. After plans were presented, the students were given actual raw performance data for the case; they prepared a profile of results and led a class discussion about interpretation.

This format afforded students several opportunities for learning and growth. The case study approach and the format in which it was used provided students an opportunity to work collaboratively in problem solving through a case. Group members interacted with each other, with their classmates, and with the instructor as well as with the material to develop and expand their problem-solving skills. The format also helped them to see that a variety of procedures can be used to address critical assessment questions because the procedures they included in their plans were not always the ones used in the actual appraisal. That particular discrepancy provided substantial opportunity for discussion that focused on strategies for obtaining relevant information. As a result of this preclinical experience, students entered their diagnostic practicum with a viable framework for approaching assessment activities.

FEATURES OF THE CASEFILES *COMPUTER PROGRAM*

The final format of *CaseFiles* varies from the teaching materials used by the author in the past, primarily with the introduction of an interactive computer program for working with the cases. The program is intended to simulate the process of assessment planning. However, both planning information and outcome data are available to students, and the gradual feeding of information does not work with the computer program as it did with distribution of hard copy data. Although it is difficult to control access to outcome data, students should work through the planning process for any case before working with actual outcomes.

Appraisal outcome data is available to read on screen or to print out from the computer program. The data are presented as raw scores and observations. The intent is that students complete the raw score interpretation. In contrast, the appraisal results printed in this *Instructor's Supplement* include the full complement of test scores and provide interpretation statements. Faculty may use their discretion whether to supply the appraisal results in this *Instructor's Supplement* to their students.

It is important that students review the "*CaseFiles* Help" section of the computer program before starting to work on the cases. This section of the program describes strategies for navigating, making choices, and printing plans and outcomes, and a preliminary review will make it easier to work through the cases. Although reviewing "*CaseFiles* Help" is important before working on all sections of the cases, it is essential for the "Appraisal Plan" sections. Design of a decision tree for the appraisal plan had to be complex due to the many branches in the decision-making process; the decision tree actually reflects the complexity of the planning process. However, the logic of the tree is explained and demonstrated in *"CaseFiles* Help." Understanding the structure before starting the program will save students from confusion as they work through the appraisal plans for each case.

A few words are in order about the *CaseFiles* program. The program cannot be run from the floppy disk; students will need to load the program onto their computer's hard disk. At least 3 MB of disk space will need to be available.

OVERVIEW OF CASES

The cases included in *CaseFiles* were selected to represent an array of ages as well as a variety of issues frequently encountered in assessing children with suspected language disorders. A brief description of each case and the rationale for including it in *CaseFiles* will help faculty decide which cases are most relevant for their instructional purposes.

- Bee is a four-year, four-month-old Hmong boy who was referred by his Head Start teacher because of concerns about his language development in both Hmong and English. Bee's case was included in *CaseFiles* to enable students to address preschool language issues as well as multicultural concerns. While it could be argued that including a case that reflects Hispanic or African-American cultural background would be more desirable for teaching students the specifics of assessing children from linguistic and cultural backgrounds that are different from their own, Bee was selected expressly because few clinicians know much about the Hmong culture or language. Consequently, students can focus on the process of assessing linguistically and culturally different children rather than on particular procedures used with children from specific cultural or linguistic backgrounds.

- Travis is a five-year, nine-month-old boy who was referred by his parents because of questions about his communication skills, in particular his inappropriate responses in conversation. Previously, Travis had been diagnosed with an attention deficit hyperactivity disorder (ADHD). Travis's case was included in *CaseFiles* to enable students to address language issues related to school entry and pragmatics as well as issues associated with ADHD. Documentation associated with Travis's case includes extensive medical records. Although some clinicians do not find review of such records illuminating, in Travis's case, medical records document the diagnosis and treatment of his attention deficit. These records also highlight frequent minor mishaps that are often seen in children with ADHD.

- Lisa is an 11-year, 8-month-old girl who was referred by her parents because of poor school achievement. Lisa has an extensive medical history, and she has missed considerable amounts of school due to severe asthma. Lisa's case was included to enable students to address language issues for upper elementary age students and to understand the impact of missed learning experiences on language function. Documentation associated with Lisa's case includes extensive educational and medical records. This documentation will provide students with a broader view of Lisa's background. With respect to educational history, the records document Lisa's achievement as well as her numerous absences from school. Her medical records illustrate the nature and severity of her asthma. These records, along with interview data, demonstrate the impact of long-term illness on Lisa's development and achievement.

- Adam is a 14-year, 10-month-old boy who was referred by his mother because of deteriorating school achievement since his entry into high school. Adam has a history of reading problems that dates to his years in elementary school. His case was included in *CaseFiles* to enable students to address adolescent language issues as well as the relationship between spoken and written language. Documentation associated with Adam's case includes medical and educational records. Because Adam has been essentially healthy, the educational materials will be more illuminating for students than the medical records. However, both sets of documentation will provide students with a broad view of Adam's background.

CaseFiles was created with a commitment to clinical teaching. It is hoped that this teaching-learning material is useful as students develop clinical problem-solving skills in assessment of children with suspected language disorders.

BEE

Language Disorder versus Language Difference

BACKGROUND INFORMATION

Background information was obtained through a telephone interview with Bee's teacher from Head Start and from a personal interview with Bee's father. The home visitor from Head Start served as the interpreter during the interview with Bee's father.

Identification and Statement of the Problem

Bee is a four-year, four-month-old boy. He lives with his mother, his father, and his five brothers.

Bee was referred for evaluation by the staff of Head Start. They were concerned about Bee's language development in Hmong and in English. At school, Bee appeared to have difficulty comprehending in both languages, and he rarely talked in either language in the school setting. When he did talk, he mouthed words and used a soft voice.

Bee's father was not concerned about Bee's communication skills. However, when Bee's teacher mentioned possible problems, he was willing to have Bee evaluated. Although he does not believe there is anything wrong with Bee, he respects the opinion of Bee's teacher. If Bee has a problem, he wants to do whatever is necessary to help him overcome it.

As an outcome of the current evaluation, Bee's father is interested in finding out if anything needs to be done to ensure Bee's success in the American school system. The Head Start staff members are interested in finding out if Bee demonstrates a language disorder and in obtaining appropriate services if necessary. They would also like suggestions for ways to help Bee in the classroom.

General Development

Pre-, para-, and perinatal history were uneventful. Although Bee's father did not provide ages at which Bee achieved various developmental milestones, he believed Bee's development was similar to that demonstrated by his older brothers. In addition,

Bee does not have difficulty with drooling, chewing, swallowing or drinking, and he makes normal sounding noise when he laughs and cries.

Medical History

Bee had ear infections during his first three months of life. These were treated with antibiotics, and no long-term problems associated with these early ear infections were mentioned. No ear infections were noted after Bee was three months of age until he began school in the fall of 1991. Examination by the school nurse at Head Start indicated that Bee had signs of middle ear infection, and it was recommended that Bee be seen by his doctor. In a subsequent medical examination, signs of ear infection were not found. However, the physician agreed that Bee may have been experiencing occasional ear infections, and he prescribed some medication. Bee's father was unsure of the type of medication, but since last fall, no other indicators of middle ear infection have been noticed. Bee has not had any other significant medical problems.

Educational History

Bee began Head Start this past fall. He attends that program five days per week from 9:00 a.m. until 2:30 p.m. At the time that Bee began school, his father saw him as happy in school and doing well, but his teacher described Bee as unresponsive much of the time. Although he entered the classroom willingly, he would not take his coat off and he rarely interacted with other children or adults. Efforts to increase Bee's responsiveness involved talking to him in Hmong. Bee's teacher interpreted his unresponsiveness as difficulty understanding language. The classroom assistant, who is Hmong, did not think Bee was understanding either English or Hmong. Bee rarely produced words in any language at school. When Bee did speak, he appeared to be mouthing words because he used such a soft voice. Approximately three weeks ago, the Head Start Home Visitor, who is Hmong, came into the classroom and began to play with Bee. He encouraged Bee to take his coat off, and in the past two to three weeks, Bee has begun to interact more with other children as well as adults at school.

Other than his unresponsiveness, Bee has not had major problems in the Head Start program. During snack time, however, he had become distracted, wanting to play with the other children, and ate slowly. As a result, his teacher separated him from the other children. She did not notice any problems related to chewing or swallowing during snack. In the classroom environment, instruction is provided in English with translation into Hmong as needed. During instructional tasks, language is contextually embedded, but general classroom discourse is decontextualized.

Social, Emotional, and Behavioral History

Bee's family came to the United States eight years ago. Before coming to the United States, Bee's parents and his two oldest siblings were in Ban Vinai, a refugee camp in Thailand close to the Lao border. Bee's parents were teenagers when they left Laos at the end of the Vietnam War. They met and married in Ban Vinai. The family came to the United States under the sponsorship of a church group in Indiana, and they lived in that state for a brief period when they first arrived in this country. Shortly after arriving, they moved to Madison, Wisconsin, where several of Bee's father's relatives lived. Three years ago, the family moved to Menomonie, Wisconsin, to be closer to other family members.

Bee has five brothers, four of whom are older than Bee. Several relatives live nearby, but Bee's family does not share its home with any other family members. Bee's older brothers are 10, 9, 7, and 6 years old; all are in school and none demonstrate any academic problems. Bee's younger brother is now 7 months old; he was born close to the time Bee began Head Start last fall. At that time, Bee was upset about having to share his father with his baby brother. When Bee found out that he could no longer sleep with his father, he stopped talking to anyone for a long period of time. Recently, Bee has begun to talk more at home. This happened after Bee's father explained to him that he still loves Bee even though there is a new baby in the family. Currently, Bee gets along well with all of his brothers and seems to like the baby.

Bee's father is a student at the University. He went to school in Laos for two or three years, and he understands and speaks but does not read or write Lao. During his years in Ban Vinai, he studied English as well as Thai, and he speaks, reads, and writes both of those languages. He does not read or write Hmong. Although he understands and speaks English well enough to accomplish his daily activities in school, he felt more comfortable having an interpreter present for the assessment of Bee. Bee's mother is a homemaker. She did not have any formal educational experiences in Laos or in the refugee camp, and she is a monolingual speaker of Hmong. She does not read or write that language.

During the week, when Bee is not at school, he spends his time at home with his mother and his baby brother. In the late afternoon and on weekends, his older brothers are also at home. On weekends, the family usually visits with relatives or friends. Bee enjoys playing with trucks and blocks. He also enjoys physical activities outside with his brothers.

Bee was described as shy. It usually takes him a while to get used to new people, and he is hesitant to talk if his father is not present. He was also described as stubborn: Bee tends to withdraw and pout when he doesn't get his own way.

Speech, Language, and Hearing History

Bee's father did not provide information about the ages at which Bee achieved speech and language developmental milestones in Hmong. However, in his home environment, Bee appears to understand and speak Hmong better than his older siblings did when they were Bee's age. His production of Hmong is usually clear, and he uses tonal aspects of the Hmong language appropriately. No concern was expressed about Bee's ability to hear.

Bee appears to understand simple commands in English, such as "Give me the _____." He produces very few single English words and does not produce complete English sentences at this time. When Bee is at home, he speaks Hmong with his parents. When Bee's older brothers speak to him in English, he responds either in Hmong or with single-word utterances in English. When relatives or other friends visit Bee's family, he speaks Hmong with the children. In general, he is shy and hesitant to speak to adults without his parents. Before beginning school six months ago, Bee did not speak any English.

The primary language used in Bee's home is Hmong. Although his father speaks English, Bee's mother speaks only Hmong. Bee's older brothers have learned English in school, and they speak that language as well as Hmong with each other in the home. They speak Hmong with their parents and both Hmong and English when they interact with Bee.

The family does not own a television. Bee is exposed to English through television programs only on occasions when he visits other family members or friends who have a television. Although Bee's parents do not read to him in any language, they tell traditional Hmong folktales, legends, and stories, and Bee enjoys hearing them. Bee's father would like Bee to learn English so he can succeed in America. However, he would also like Bee to maintain his Hmong heritage.

APPRAISAL PLANS AND OUTCOMES

Following is the appraisal decision tree broken down visually by domain and target. Following the appraisal decision tree segments are the appraisal outcomes for Bee.

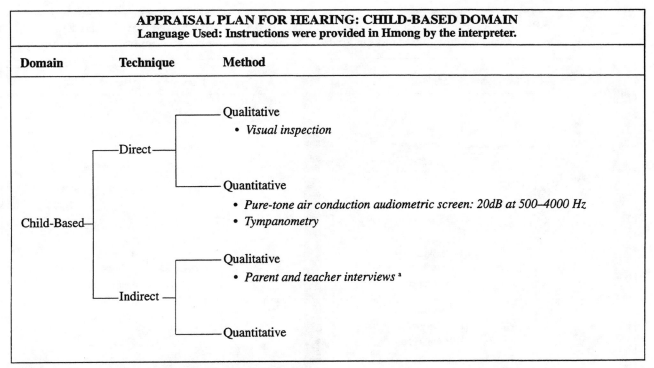

APPRAISAL PLAN FOR HEARING: CHILD-BASED DOMAIN
Language Used: Instructions were provided in Hmong by the interpreter.

Domain	Technique	Method

Child-Based

Direct
- Qualitative
  - *Visual inspection*
- Quantitative
  - *Pure-tone air conduction audiometric screen: 20dB at 500–4000 Hz*
  - *Tympanometry*

Indirect
- Qualitative
  - *Parent and teacher interviews* [a]
- Quantitative

[a] The parent interview was conducted with the assistance of an interpreter.

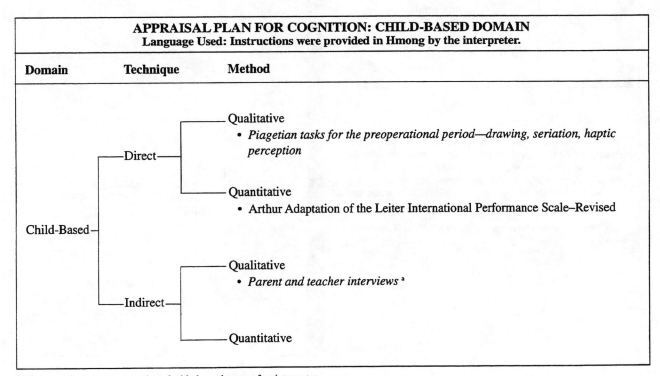

APPRAISAL PLAN FOR COGNITION: CHILD-BASED DOMAIN
Language Used: Instructions were provided in Hmong by the interpreter.

Domain	Technique	Method

Child-Based

Direct
- Qualitative
  - *Piagetian tasks for the preoperational period—drawing, seriation, haptic perception*
- Quantitative
  - Arthur Adaptation of the Leiter International Performance Scale–Revised

Indirect
- Qualitative
  - *Parent and teacher interviews* [a]
- Quantitative

[a] The parent interview was conducted with the assistance of an interpreter.

APPRAISAL PLAN FOR LANGUAGE: CHILD-BASED DOMAIN, BASIC LEVEL

Language Used: The clinician administered tasks in English; the interpreter administered equivalent tasks in Hmong.

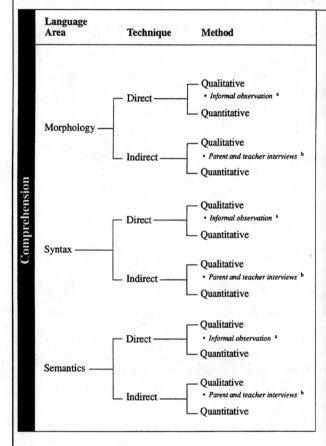

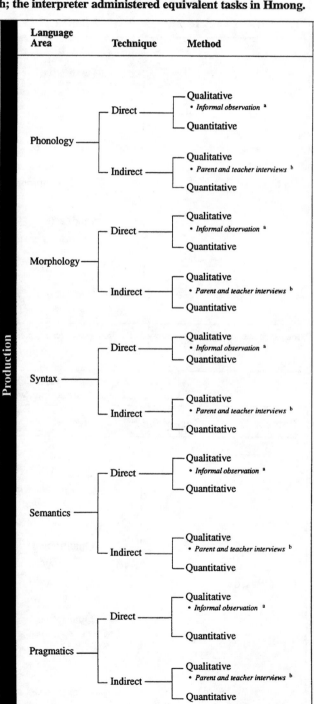

[a] Equivalent informal tasks were used for the two languages, Hmong and English. Tasks included requests for personal identifying information, following verbal directions with and without gestures, identifying and labeling common objects, and giving functions. Materials used included Fischer-Price farm and animals, bubbles, and assorted toys.

[b] The parent interview was conducted with the assistance of an interpreter.

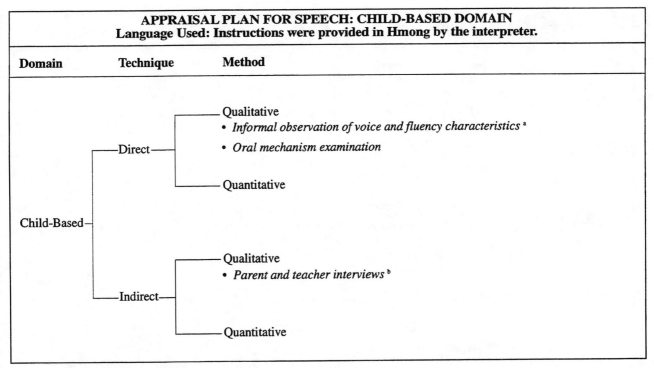

APPRAISAL PLAN FOR SPEECH: CHILD-BASED DOMAIN
Language Used: Instructions were provided in Hmong by the interpreter.

Domain	Technique	Method

Child-Based — Direct — Qualitative
• *Informal observation of voice and fluency characteristics* [a]
• *Oral mechanism examination*
Quantitative

Indirect — Qualitative
• *Parent and teacher interviews* [b]
Quantitative

[a] Both Hmong and English were appraised.

[b] The parent interview was conducted with the assistance of an interpreter.

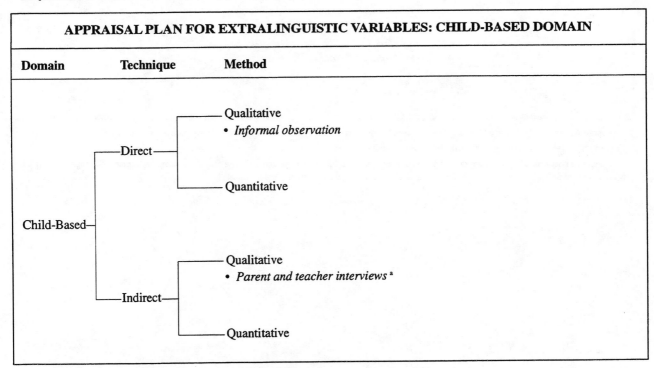

APPRAISAL PLAN FOR EXTRALINGUISTIC VARIABLES: CHILD-BASED DOMAIN

Domain	Technique	Method

Child-Based — Direct — Qualitative
• *Informal observation*
Quantitative

Indirect — Qualitative
• *Parent and teacher interviews* [a]
Quantitative

[a] The parent interview was conducted with the assistance of an interpreter.

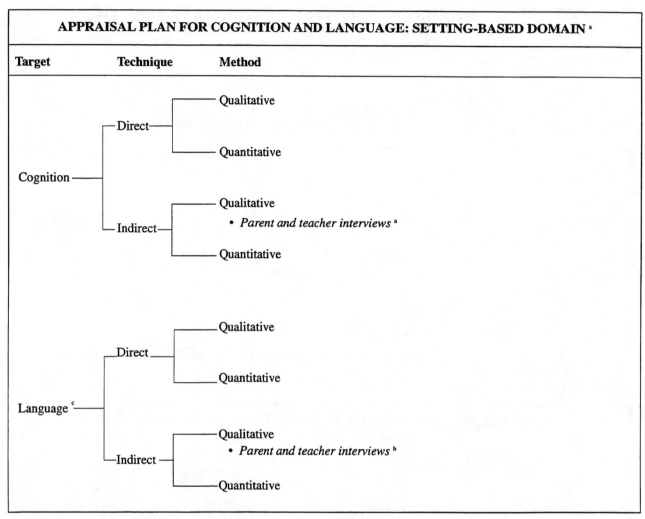

APPRAISAL PLAN FOR COGNITION AND LANGUAGE: SETTING-BASED DOMAIN [a]

Target	Technique	Method
Cognition	Direct	Qualitative
		Quantitative
	Indirect	Qualitative • *Parent and teacher interviews* [a]
		Quantitative
Language [c]	Direct	Qualitative
		Quantitative
	Indirect	Qualitative • *Parent and teacher interviews* [b]
		Quantitative

[a] An appraisal plan was determined to be necessary for the setting-based domain—hearing, speech, and extralinguistic variables targets.

[b] The parent interview was conducted with the assistance of an interpreter.

[c] The language functions of comprehension and production and the language areas of phonology, morphology, syntax, semantics, and pragmatics have been combined in this simple variation of the appraisal decision tree. Basic language level is assumed.

APPRAISAL OUTCOMES: CHILD-BASED DOMAIN

HEARING

RESULTS

Pure-tone screen	Failed bilaterally at 20 dB at 500–4000 Hz
Tympanometry	Negative middle ear pressure bilaterally
Visual inspection	Retracted ear drums bilaterally
Parent and teacher interviews	See Background Information about Bee in this *Instructor's Supplement* or in the Interview Outcomes in the *CaseFiles* computer program.

INTERPRETATION   Hearing test results suggest existence of possible middle ear pathology. Bee's history of middle ear infection and uncertainty about his hearing status raise questions about the adequacy of his hearing to support classroom activities. Although speculative, it may be that Bee has been experiencing chronic middle ear infections and associated chronically reduced air conduction acuity. If this is true, it would suggest possible contributors to his soft voice and his poor attention in school.

COGNITION

RESULTS [a]

Piagetian tasks for the preoperational period

- Drawing   Bee accurately copied a plus sign (+), circle, and square. This performance is commensurate with expectations for children between four and four and a half years of age.

- Seriation   Bee showed trial-and-error strategy, but was successful with five cylinders; he correctly inserted two more cylinders. This performance is commensurate with expectations for children between four and four and a half years of age.

- Haptic perception   Bee differentiated circles and squares, but he had difficulty distinguishing types of shapes with angles (e.g., square, triangle, rectangle) from types of shapes without angles (e.g., circle, ellipse).

Arthur Adaptation of the Leiter International Performance Scale–Revised

- Two-year tests   Passed all tests
- Three-year tests   Passed all tests
- Four-year tests   Passed all tests
- Five-year tests   Passed one test

     Passing all two-, three-, and four-year tests on the *Leiter* yields a mental age of four years, three months. Passing one test at the five-year level adds another three months. Results suggest an overall mental age of four years, six months.

(continued)

Parent and teacher interviews	See Background Information about Bee in this *Instructor's Supplement* or in the Interview Outcomes in the *CaseFiles* computer program.

[a] All tasks were administered in Hmong with the assistance of an interpreter.

INTERPRETATION	Results on these relatively language-free cognitive tasks suggest that Bee's thinking skills are age appropriate and adequate to support language function.

LANGUAGE

RESULTS: BASIC LEVEL

COMPREHENSION AND PRODUCTION

	Hmong Performances	**English Performances**
Informal observation		
• Semantics	Bee performed simple actions on objects (e.g., touch your foot) when engaged in play. Bee labeled common objects (e.g., ball, shoe) and, speaking Hmong, told the examiner the functions of the objects. In Hmong, he identified and named several colors, shapes, and qualitative characteristics of objects.	Even with overt gestures, Bee did not follow simple directions (e.g., walk to the door). Bee spontaneously named one of four objects in English (ball), and he spontaneously named the functions of two of four objects in English (ball → play, chair → sit) with single-word utterances. He did not identify or name any colors, shapes, or qualitative characteristics of objects in English.
• Morphology and Syntax	Bee used full sentences in interaction with his father and the interpreter. Linguistic characteristics of Hmong were judged to be normal by the interpreter.	In a play situation with the examiner, Bee primarily spoke Hmong. However, he frequently imitated the examiner's use of English and occasionally spoke English spontaneously using single-word utterances.
• Phonology	Bee accurately imitated Hmong words produced by the interpreter that differed only in tonal characteristics. In Hmong, conversational productions were judged by the interpreter to be accurate and normal with respect to phonemic segments and tones.	Bee produced the following single words in imitation of the examiner: • boats [boʊs] • fork [foʊk] • glasses [gæs] • gum [gʌ] • leaf [jif] • rock [wɑk] • soap [soʊp] • spoon [spum] • star [tɑr] • watch [wɑts] • zipper [zɪpə]

Appraisal Outcomes: Child-Based Domain—*Continued*		
• Pragmatics	Bee talked frequently in Hmong to his father, the interpreter, and the clinician. He did not respond to requests for personal identifying information (e.g., What is your name? How old are you?). When playing with his father and the interpreter, Bee did not use any English. During this time, he commented on the actions of others, attended to the speaker, requested attention, expressed his needs and feelings, took turns talking, initiated conversations, maintained topics, and answered questions; he did not comment on his own actions, request information, or request action.	Bee interacted freely with the examiner, but he did not answer any questions about himself presented in English. Bee did not spontaneously use words like *more, open,* or *blow* while playing with bubbles with the examiner. However he pretended to blow as a nonverbal request for continuation. While playing with the examiner, Bee commented on other's actions, requested information, requested action, expressed his needs, took turns, and maintained topics using nonverbal communication and occasional single-word English utterances.
Parent and teacher interviews	See Background Information about Bee in this *Instructor's Supplement* or in the Interview Outcomes in the *CaseFiles* computer program.	
INTERPRETATION	Bee's language skills in Hmong appear to be within normal limits, but his skills in English are limited. This discrepancy in relative language skill supports a decision of language difference, not language disorder. This finding is in agreement with information derived from the parent interview, but it is at odds with information derived from the teacher interview.	

SPEECH

RESULTS

Informal observation

• Voice characteristics	Bee used a soft voice in Hmong and English during most of the evaluation, but he increased intensity when asked to do so. He consistently spoke more loudly in Hmong than in English.
• Fluency characteristics	Bee's fluency characteristics were unremarkable in both Hmong and English.
Oral mechanism examination	Instructions for the oral mechanism examination were provided in Hmong by the interpreter. Bee did not cooperate with the oral mechanism examination. During snack, however, he was able to bite, chew, and swallow adequately; no drooling was noted. Facial features appeared symmetrical.
Parent and teacher interviews	See Background Information about Bee in this *Instructor's Supplement* or in the Interview Outcomes in the *CaseFiles* computer program.
INTERPRETATION	Bee's speech characteristics appear to be within normal limits. His use of soft voice may be related to his hearing status. His tendency to speak more loudly in Hmong than in English may be related to greater facility and comfort in using his native language.

(continued)

Appraisal Outcomes: Child-Based Domain—*Continued*

EXTRALINGUISTIC VARIABLES

RESULTS

Informal observation | Bee engaged readily in play with the examiner, demonstrating focused joint attention on the farm and bubble toys. Bee and the examiner were actively playing with bubbles before his father and the interpreter entered the room. When Bee's father and the interpreter began to ask Bee preplanned evaluation questions in Hmong, Bee refused to answer, sitting quietly on the floor with his head bowed. Bee persistently ignored repeated requests and commands in Hmong to do as he was told. He appeared upset that the bubbles were taken away, and he seemed uninterested in doing the tasks requested of him. When the setting was changed to a more informal play situation, Bee readily interacted with his father and the interpreter, performing tasks requested.

Parent and teacher interviews | See Background Information about Bee in this *Instructor's Supplement* or in the Interview Outcomes in the *CaseFiles* computer program.

INTERPRETATION

Bee's attention appeared to be within normal limits. However, his stubbornness surfaced when the task was not to his liking. Bee's behavior was congruent with descriptions provided by his father and his teacher during interviews.

APPRAISAL OUTCOMES: SETTING-BASED DOMAIN

COGNITION

Based on information derived from the parent and teacher interviews, the cognitive demands placed on Bee at home appear to be congruent with his developmental level. At school, however, although cognitive demands are congruent with his developmental level, the primarily English environment confounds Bee's ability to demonstrate his true skills.

LANGUAGE

Based on information derived from the parent and teacher interviews, the language demands in Bee's home appear to be congruent with his abilities. Although Hmong is the primary language of the home, Bee is also exposed to some English in that environment. In addition, Bee is free to respond in Hmong or in English, and specific demands for response language are not made. In contrast, language demands in school are primarily in English. Moreover, language may be decontextualized. While these demands may not place undue stress on children who are fluent speakers of English, for Bee the school language demands are excessive. Furthermore, the language demands of the school environment do not seem to account adequately for Bee's status as a learner of English as a second language. In that regard, school staff seem unaware of the phases of second language learning and the affective aspects of communicating in a nonnative language. In general, the language demands of the school setting interfere with Bee's ability to function adequately in that environment.

SUGGESTED DISCUSSION ISSUES

Does Bee demonstrate a language disorder?

From a diagnostic decision-making perspective, addressing this issue can be approached most productively by leading students through Damico's (1991) descriptive assessment and explanatory analysis strategies. Descriptive assessment involves observation and analysis of communication as it functions holistically in naturalistic contexts. Such an assessment is reflected in the actual outcomes presented for Bee. If problem areas are suggested from descriptive observation and analysis, those problem areas are then subjected to explanatory analysis, which seeks to determine why problem behaviors may exist.

In Damico's formulation, explanations attempt to distinguish factors that are extrinsic to the child from intrinsic learning deficits. Application of explanatory analysis with children from linguistic and cultural minority backgrounds demands that the evaluator assume problem behaviors are due to extrinsic factors until such factors can be eliminated as possible explanations. Extrinsic versus intrinsic distinctions are made by addressing several questions:

• *Do any overt variables, such as limited exposure to English or substantial inconsistencies in performance across contexts, immediately explain the communicative difficulties in English?* In Bee's case, the answer to this question is yes. Bee was referred for evaluation during the fall of his first semester in the Head Start program. At that time, he had been exposed to English on a casual basis, primarily through interactions with his brothers. At the time of the assessment, he had been in Head Start for only eight months. Even given daily attendance in that program, his formal exposure to English was still limited. In addition, inconsistencies in Bee's performances were reported and observed across contexts. Although he continued to demonstrate minimal language usage in school at the time of the evaluation, at home he showed acceptable levels of language use. During the evaluation, he demonstrated consistently high levels of language usage. Moreover, he consistently demonstrates ignoring behaviors at school, but not at home. During the appraisal, ignoring behaviors were noted only when he appeared displeased with activities.

• *Does the child show the same types of problematic behaviors in both the native language and in English?* For Bee, the answer to this question is no. During the assessment, Bee responded to and used his native language appropriately and well. Although he interacted appropriately under English conditions, he responded to and used English minimally.

• *Can the problematic behaviors noted in English be explained as reflecting normal second language acquisition or dialect variations?* For Bee, the answer to this question is yes. Cummins (1981, 1984) distinguished social and academic types of language proficiency and described these skills as existing on a continuum from context-embedded to context-reduced situational demands. Children must develop language skills all along the continuum to function adequately academically. Yet Cummins (1981) estimated that it takes the average child 2 years of instructed learning to develop social communication skills and an additional 5 to 7 years to develop academic communication skills. Other researchers (Collier and Thomas, 1989) have found that children from literate cultures with a history of educational achievement in their first language take between 7 and 10 years to develop academic communication skills and achieve at grade level. Clearly, Bee is still within the window of acquisition of basic social communication skills for English.

Bee's performances can also be understood in terms of phases of social-type language development in second language learning. The early stages of second language learning are often characterized by a silent period (Johns, 1988; Saville-Troike, 1987). In this silent period, the child typically withdraws from interaction and focuses his energies on listening and observing. Although silence was not noted during the appraisal, Bee's behaviors at school may reflect features of the silent period. In addition, in normal second language acquisition, the silent period is typically followed by reinitiation of verbal interactions with speakers of the second language. During this phase, utterances are typically one to two words in length, and single words are usually the names of objects (Johns, 1988). Bee demonstrated Phase II behaviors during the appraisal, and his teacher indicated some increase in his verbal interactions at school.

• *Can the problematic behaviors noted in English be explained as reflecting cross-cultural interference or other culturally grounded phenomena?* For Bee, the answer to this question is maybe. As in all cultures, Hmong children are taught specific culturally conditioned behaviors, and these behaviors have implications for assessment personnel. For example, in the Hmong culture, children are taught to be submissive, unassertive, polite, obedient, and modest (Bliatout, Downing, Lewis, and Yang, 1988). Such behavioral expectations are in line with cultural values that focus on the group rather than on the individual (McInnis, Petracchi, and Morgenbesser, 1990), and such culturally conditioned learning surfaces in a number of observable behaviors. In classroom situations, Hmong children engage in little class participation. They are unlikely to ask questions or to volunteer ideas. Rather, they tend to listen quietly. Bee's behavior at school may reflect culturally grounded behavior, although it is difficult to tell how traditionally oriented his family is and the degree to which his silence reflects culturally conditioned values.

• *Can the problematic behaviors noted in English be explained as reflecting bias that may have been operating before, during, or after descriptive analysis?* For Bee, the answer to this question is also maybe. The degree of bias influencing Bee's teacher's observations of him in the classroom is unknown. Although she has had some experience with Hmong children, her observations and interpretations may be colored by inappropriate cultural expectations. In addition, while efforts were made to reduce bias both during the assessment itself and during interpretation, the possibility of such bias always exists.

These initial questions focus on extrinsic factors. If they cannot explain the observed problematic behaviors then the child may, indeed, have an intrinsic language-learning disability and a final question must be addressed:

- *Is there evidence of underlying linguistic systematicity to the observed problematic behaviors?* According to Damico, many children will not need the detailed linguistic analysis demanded by the final question because their difficulties will be explained by extrinsic factors. Clearly this is the case with Bee: it would appear that extrinsic factors can explain his behaviors. Thus, it is unlikely that he demonstrates an intrinsic language-learning disorder.

From a theory-to-practice perspective, the question of whether or not Bee demonstrates a language disorder highlights issues about definitions of language disorder. Addressing this question forces students to think critically about elements included in theoretically driven statements about language disorders and how those statements play out in practice. In that regard, consideration could be given to how various theories of language account for the typically followed definition of language disorder in multicultural populations. Recall that to judge children from non-English language backgrounds as disordered, problems must cut across all languages. Is this definition grounded legally, theoretically, or both? Moreover, on a practical level, the typically followed definition requires appraising relative skills with equivalent tasks in all languages. Addressing this issue will help students think critically about task selection and design in appraisal planning.

What predictions can be made about Bee's future language learning and use?

Although this question focuses on the prognostic phase of the assessment-intervention process, it also offers opportunities to address information about second language acquisition processes and patterns. Such an issue links theory to practice by considering the universality of language-learning processes and mechanisms, and by helping students consider variations in first and second language learning. In Bee's case, it is reasonable to predict that his use of English will emerge normally over time, following typical learning patterns for a second language.

What recommendations should be made for Bee?

Speech and language intervention is clearly not indicated for Bee. However, some feedback should be provided to his teacher. Students should consider the kinds of information and suggestions to offer her for understanding Bee and helping him in the classroom. For example, enabling the teacher to learn more about normal first and second language acquisition patterns as well as oral-literate language distinctions will help her with respect to Bee and other Hmong students in the future. In addition, students should consider ways to help the teacher help Bee on an affective level. In that regard, it might be useful to help the teacher develop different communication styles with Bee.

Although direct intervention is not indicated for Bee's speech and language skills, his hearing requires some attention. Students should consider the implications of the direct hearing assessment results and recommendations associated with those findings.

What skills and attitudes are involved in using interpreters in assessment?

In large measure, this is a practical question that will help students focus on the logistics of using an interpreter throughout the evaluation. In particular, the need for planning and collaboration with the interpreter before, during, and after the appraisal should be highlighted. Debriefing discussion might also address students' potential discomfort in relying on indirect data and someone else's judgment about children's skills and abilities. A number of theory-to-practice issues also can be addressed through this question. For example, the impact on child performances and diagnostic decisions of appraising a language in which the clinician is not fluent could be considered as well as the problems inherent in translating language tasks from one language to another.

What is the relative utility of qualitative versus quantitative methods with Bee?

This question offers opportunities for students to think critically about various appraisal methods. In the actual appraisal plan for Bee, most of the tasks used were informal and qualitative in nature. Given that observation, discussion could address problems inherent in the use of norm-referenced materials with multicultural populations as well as the reliability and validity of observational data. In addition, discussion might address the reference standards used for informal observation and their applicability to multicultural populations. Such discussion can facilitate students' critical thinking about normative data.

What differences were noted in students' interview and appraisal plans and those actually implemented in the assessment of Bee?

Students' plans may differ from those actually used in the assessment of Bee. For example, students may have chosen direct as well as indirect techniques for appraising setting-based aspects of Bee's cognitive and communication skills. Debriefing on these differences can help students see that there are numerous ways of approaching assessment of children with suspected language disorders.

These issues could also spark a discussion of the speech-language pathologist's role with respect to teachers and other professionals. For the teacher, students may consider a consultation relationship. In that regard, discussion could address the bi-directional nature of consultation and the ways in which speech-language pathologists can function on transdisciplinary teams. In addition, many Head Start programs employ speech-language pathologists; this point offers opportunities to discuss development of inter- and intradisciplinary communication lines.

TRAVIS

ADHD versus Language Disorder

BACKGROUND INFORMATION

Background information was obtained from a case history form. Additionally, background information was obtained from an interview with Travis's mother.

Identification and Statement of the Problem

Travis is a five-year, nine-month-old boy. He lives with his mother, his father, and his three siblings.

Travis was referred for evaluation by his mother. She was concerned about his inappropriate responses in conversation and questioned whether they were due to delayed receptive language skills, poor language processing, or to distractions related to Travis's attention deficit hyperactivity disorder. The problem was first noticed when Travis was about four years old. The family sought assistance for Travis's suspected attention problems from their pediatrician and a child psychologist. They contacted the special education

service in their local school district for evaluation of Travis's suspected language disorder. The school psychologist suggested that the family bring Travis to the University's Center for Communication Disorders for evaluation before pursuing an assessment by school district personnel. Travis's mother was not sure why this recommendation was made.

Travis does not respond appropriately when interacting with conversational partners. He often responds with a comment that is unrelated to the current situation. This occurs at least once or twice a day and tends to interfere with people being able to understand Travis. Travis does not appear to understand why others do not understand him. He seems to think the problem is not caused by him, but by the listener.

As an outcome of the current evaluation, Travis's parents hope to gain a greater understanding of his language abilities. They also hope to achieve insight into how his attention and language skills may influence his academic performance when he begins school.

General Development

Pre-, para-, and perinatal history were uneventful. In general, developmental milestones were within normal limits. Travis's parents were not concerned about the relatively late age at which he achieved bowel and bladder control, and he has maintained consistent control since he was 50 months of age.

Medical History

Travis's parents noted only three significant medical events on the case history form. Travis had a moderate case of chicken pox at two years of age; he did not experience any complications with this illness. He also suffered a temperature of 104° F for 48 hours. This was associated with "strep blood sepsis," but no complications followed his illness. Travis's age at the time of this illness was unclear. Travis was diagnosed with attention deficit hyperactivity disorder (ADHD) when he was about four-and-a-half years old. He is currently taking 10 mg. of Ritalin three times a day for this problem. He has not shown any negative side-effects to the medication, and his parents have noticed substantial improvement in his behavior since the initial diagnosis. (See Medical Records on pages 175–187 in *CaseFiles* for the full history.)

Educational History

Travis is currently in his second year of preschool which he attends two days a week for approximately two and one-half hours per day. The school's focus is social rather than academic, and achievement records are not available. However, Travis was screened in the prekindergarten program of his local school district and found to be above average in knowledge. The parents believed that reports from the screening would not be helpful, and they were not obtained. Travis will be entering kindergarten in the fall of this year.

Before the diagnosis of ADHD, Travis had difficulty in the preschool setting, particularly in getting along with other children and in complying with school rules. Following his diagnosis, he gets along with other children better and appears much happier. From the parents' points of view, his positive school experience in the year since the diagnosis is related more to Travis's improved behavior than to programmatic efforts by the preschool staff.

Social, Emotional, and Behavioral History

Travis lives with his parents, an older brother and sister, and a younger brother. Both of his parents work outside of the home. His father teaches math at a local high school. His mother is a registered nurse who works part-time at a local hospital. When Travis is not at preschool, he typically spends his time at home with his mother and younger brother. On the occasions when his mother works, Travis and his brother go to a baby sitter in the neighborhood. Travis gets along best with his younger brother, with whom he spends the most time when the other children are in school.

Travis's interactions with other children vary, primarily as a function of his behavior. Since being diagnosed with ADHD and beginning treatment with Ritalin, his interactions with children have improved. However, his interactions with adults continue to be poor. This is attributed to his inappropriate language and hyperactivity.

Travis was described as having a poor appetite and being a "finicky eater." This has been true since he was an infant. Although he eats his food in smaller portions than other children, he gains weight and no concerns were reported about his eating habits.

On a typical school day, Travis gets up at approximately 7:00 a.m. and has breakfast. He goes to school from 9:00 to 11:30, and he comes home for lunch. In the afternoon, he plays with his younger brother and with other neighborhood children, typically engaging in active physical play although he also enjoys playing with toy animals. The family eats dinner together between 5:00 and 6:00 p.m.; after dinner, he plays with his siblings and may watch some television. He usually has a bath and is in bed by 8:00 p.m. Although one of his parents sometimes reads to him, Travis does not enjoy listening to bedtime stories. On days when Travis does not go to school, his schedule is similar, with the exception that he plays all day rather than just in the afternoon.

On weekends, the family enjoys going to church and engaging in other group activities such as going camping, visiting museums, or seeing relatives. They have found, however, that Travis's need for a structured and consistent environment has restricted the kinds of things they can do as a total family. Although efforts to institute a behavior management program with Travis have led to a relatively more serene home environment, it is still difficult for Travis to deal with deviations from his known routine. The parents believe that improvements in the home environment are due to their efforts at structuring the setting and following a behavior management program as well as to changes in Travis as a function of taking Ritalin.

Speech, Language, and Hearing History

Speech and language developmental milestones were within normal limits, and no hearing problems were noted or discussed by his parents. Although Travis has experienced several middle ear infections (see Medical Records on pages 175–187 in *CaseFiles*), these episodes have not affected his hearing. Travis was described as a verbal and articulate child. He has a wide vocabulary and expresses his needs and wants adequately. Concern about Travis's speech, language, and hearing is driven by his language responses which are frequently inappropriate to the situation or the conversational topic. Travis tends to yell or screech to attract attention or express annoyance. This has been true since he was an infant, but his parents attribute this behavior to his attention deficit and hyperactivity; the behavior has decreased somewhat since Travis began taking Ritalin. Although Travis showed marked alertness to gesture, facial expression, and movement when he was younger, he no longer demonstrates this behavior.

APPRAISAL PLAN AND OUTCOMES

Following is the appraisal decision tree broken down visually by domain and target. Following the appraisal decision tree segments are the appraisal outcomes for Travis.

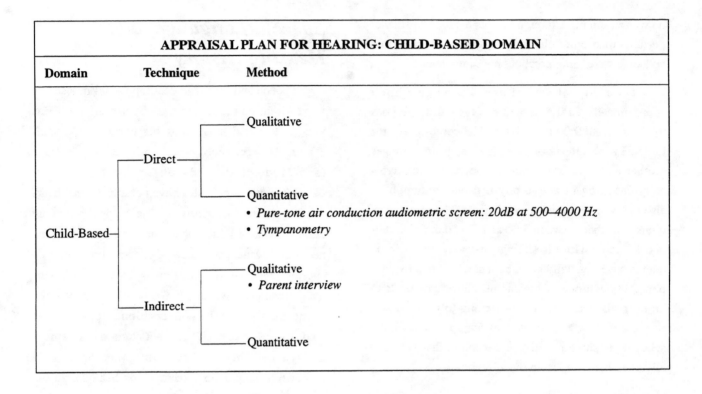

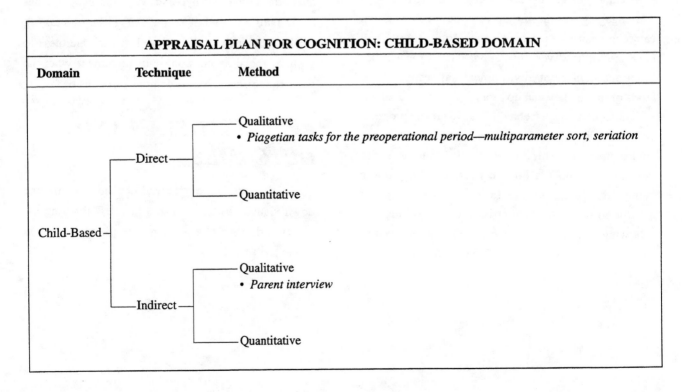

APPRAISAL PLAN FOR LANGUAGE: CHILD-BASED DOMAIN, BASIC LEVEL

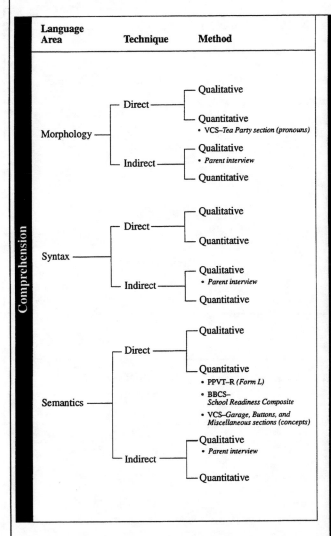

Comprehension

Language Area	Technique	Method
Morphology	Direct	Qualitative Quantitative • VCS–*Tea Party section (pronouns)*
	Indirect	Qualitative • *Parent interview* Quantitative
Syntax	Direct	Qualitative Quantitative
	Indirect	Qualitative • *Parent interview* Quantitative
Semantics	Direct	Qualitative Quantitative • PPVT–R *(Form L)* • BBCS–*School Readiness Composite* • VCS–*Garage, Buttons, and Miscellaneous sections (concepts)*
	Indirect	Qualitative • *Parent interview* Quantitative

Note: In addition to these specifications for the basic level, the plan also included administration of the *Preschool Language Assessment Instrument,* a transitional-level task designed to appraise children's ability to comprehend and use school-type language.

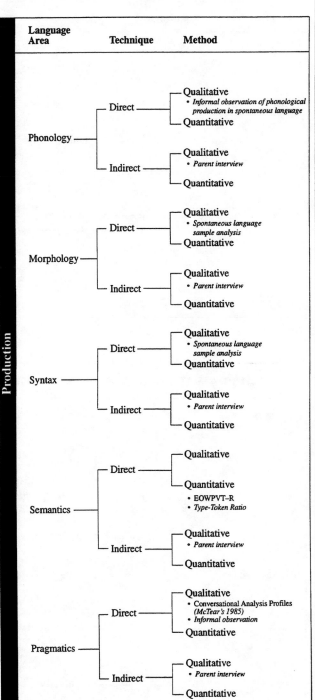

Production

Language Area	Technique	Method
Phonology	Direct	Qualitative • *Informal observation of phonological production in spontaneous language* Quantitative
	Indirect	Qualitative • *Parent interview* Quantitative
Morphology	Direct	Qualitative • *Spontaneous language sample analysis* Quantitative
	Indirect	Qualitative • *Parent interview* Quantitative
Syntax	Direct	Qualitative • *Spontaneous language sample analysis* Quantitative
	Indirect	Qualitative • *Parent interview* Quantitative
Semantics	Direct	Qualitative Quantitative • EOWPVT–R • *Type-Token Ratio*
	Indirect	Qualitative • *Parent interview* Quantitative
Pragmatics	Direct	Qualitative • Conversational Analysis Profiles *(McTear's 1985)* • *Informal observation* Quantitative
	Indirect	Qualitative • *Parent interview* Quantitative

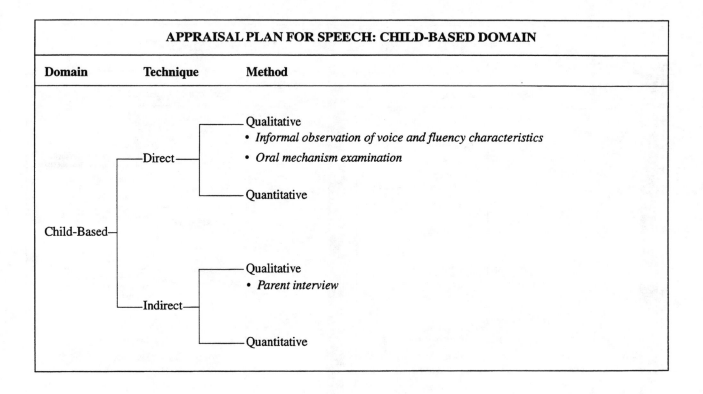

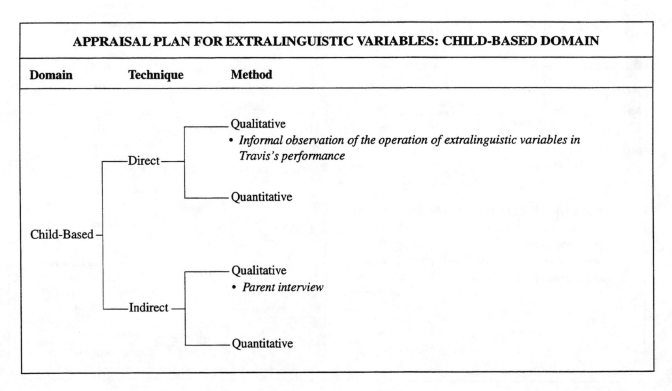

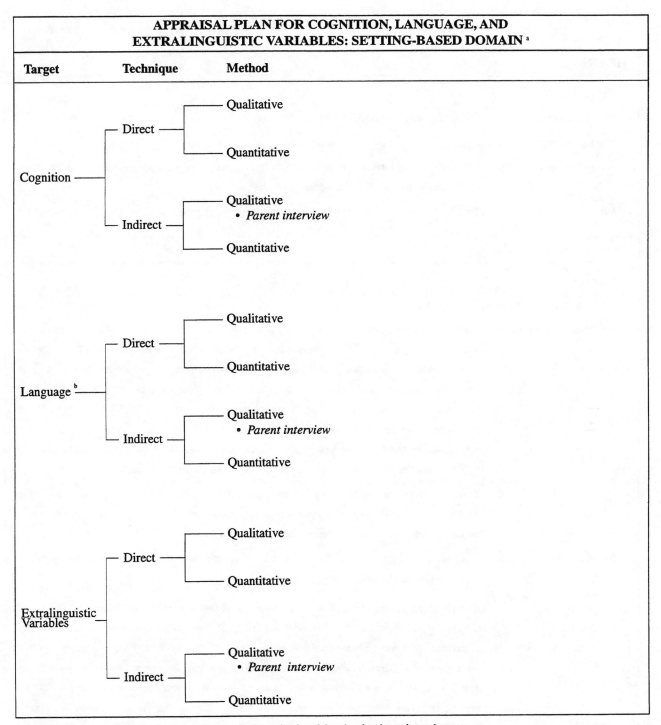

APPRAISAL PLAN FOR COGNITION, LANGUAGE, AND EXTRALINGUISTIC VARIABLES: SETTING-BASED DOMAIN [a]

[a] An appraisal plan was determined to be unnecessary for the setting-based domain—hearing and speech targets.

[b] The language functions of comprehension and production and the language areas of phonology, morphology, syntax, semantics, and pragmatics have been combined in this simple variation of the appraisal decision tree. Basic and transitional language levels are assumed.

APPRAISAL OUTCOMES: CHILD-BASED DOMAIN	
HEARING	

RESULTS

Pure-tone screen	Passed bilaterally at 20 dB at 500–4000 Hz
Tympanometry	Normal middle ear pressure bilaterally
Parent interview	See Background Information about Travis in this *Instructor's Supplement* or in the Interview Outcomes in the *CaseFiles* computer program.
INTERPRETATION	Travis's hearing appeared to be adequate for reception of speech and language.

COGNITION

RESULTS

Piagetian tasks for the preoperational period

- Multiparameter sort — Travis placed both blue and yellow blocks on each pile, but there were definite separations of color within each pile. For a rationale, he said, "They match." When asked to do it another way, he made designs, then placed yellow blocks on one pile and yellow and blue blocks on the other pile. For a rationale, he said, "They match." When probed, he explained that the blocks on the yellow pile matched "because they are the same color." With respect to the blocks on the other pile, he indicated that they matched "because they are the same color but these don't go there because they don't match," and he pulled out the yellow blocks, leaving only blue blocks. When asked to do it yet another way, he refused the task.

- Seriation — Travis did not seriate either 10 or 5 cylinders given a model. He seriated 3 cylinders given a model, and then inserted 5 more cylinders in the appropriate place. He did not appear to attend to instructional cues about the blocks forming upward steps.

Parent interview	See Background Information about Travis in this *Instructor's Supplement* or in the Interview Outcomes in the *CaseFiles* computer program.
INTERPRETATION	Results of the multiparameter sorting task suggest that Travis has classification skills, but because of his limited compliance with the task, adequacy of his performance was not fully determined. His performance on the seriation task was commensurate with performances that are typical of children between four and five years of age. However, due to his inattention, Travis's performance on both of these tasks may not accurately reflect his abilities. In that regard, Travis's mother, who watched the appraisal, indicated that Travis does not like to play with blocks and does not like to do tasks over.

(continued)

Appraisal Outcomes: Child-Based Domain—*Continued*

LANGUAGE

RESULTS: BASIC LEVEL

COMPREHENSION

Semantics

	Raw Score	Standard Score	SEM	Percentile Rank	Age Equivalent
PPVT–R (Form L) (mean standard score = 100, sd = 15)	54	88	5	22	4;9
BBCS (School Readiness Composite) (mean standard score = 10, sd = 3)	43 [a]	6	1.4 [b]	9	4;10
VCS–Garage, Buttons, and Miscellaneous sections (concepts)					scattered 3;0 to 5;6 [c]

Parent interview	See Background Information about Travis in this *Instructor's Supplement* or in the Interview Outcomes in the *CaseFiles* computer program.

Morphology

	Raw Score	Standard Score	SEM	Percentile Rank	Age Equivalent
VCS—Tea Party section (pronouns)					scattered 4;6–5;6

Parent interview	See Background Information about Travis in this *Instructor's Supplement* or in the Interview Outcomes in the *CaseFiles* computer program.

Syntax

Parent interview	See Background Information about Travis in this *Instructor's Supplement* or in the Interview Outcomes in the *CaseFiles* computer program.

PRODUCTION

Phonology

Informal observation	Inconsistent gliding of liquid /l/ (e.g., [wɛg] for /lɛg/; [wif] for /lif/) and minimal place shifts (e.g., [sʌmfɪŋ] for /sʌmθɪŋ/) were noted. Travis's speech was intelligible.
Parent interview	See Background Information about Travis in this *Instructor's Supplement* or in the Interview Outcomes in the *CaseFiles* computer program.

(continued)

Appraisal Outcomes: Child-Based Domain—*Continued*					
Semantics					
	Raw Score	**Standard Score**	**SEM**	**Percentile Rank**	**Age Equivalent**
EOWPVT–R (mean standard score = 100, sd = 15)	66	127	6.54	96	8;6

Type-Token Ratio	**Different Words**	**Total Words**	**TTR Value**	**Age Equivalent**
	119	255	.45	5;0-6;0

Parent interview — See Background Information about Travis in this *Instructor's Supplement* or in the Interview Outcomes in the *CaseFiles* computer program.

Morphology and Syntax

Spontaneous language sample analysis — Because of Travis's age, MLU-M was not calculated. However, a syntactic analysis, following procedures outlined by Retherford (1993), was conducted. Results showed that Travis used structures ranging from those most typical of a child 19–22 months of age up to a child 47–50 months of age. The amount of variability of Travis's production of morphosyntactic structures is considered acceptable, but it appears that he is using linguistic structures that are below expectations for his chronological age. However, due to Travis's limited conversational interaction, the language sample frequently involved answering questions posed by the examiner. This may have restricted his use of more syntactically complex structures.

Parent interview — See Background Information about Travis in this *Instructor's Supplement* or in the Interview Outcomes in the *CaseFiles* computer program.

Pragmatics

Conversational Analysis Profiles	**Analytic Category**	**Descriptor(s)**	**Rating**
	Turn-Taking	Gaps between turns > 5 seconds	Regularly
	Responses	No response	Regularly
		Inappropriate response	Regularly
		Minimal predicted response	Regularly
		Response + additional content	Rarely
		Other appropriate response	Rarely
	Initiations		
	• Attention-getting nonverbal devices	Eye contact Physical pointing, showing	Rarely Never
	• Attention-getting verbal devices	Present referents (Looking, pointing)	Rarely to never
		Nonpresent referents (Locating devices, relative clauses)	Rarely to never

(continued)

Appraisal Outcomes: Child-Based Domain—*Continued*

	• Types of initiations	Question	Occasionally
		Request for action	Occasionally
		Statement	Occasionally
	• Types of re-initiations	Repeats	Occasionally
		Repeats with prosodic shift	Rarely to never
		Repeats with attention-getting direction	Rarely to never
		Rephrasing	Rarely to never
	Cohesive devices	Exophoric referents	Occasionally
		Endophoric referents	Occasionally (Primarily ellipsis and contrastive stress)
		Discourse connectors	Occasionally (Primarily "and")
	Appropriacy in requests for action (Primarily direct imperatives)	Nonverbal requests	Rarely
		Verbal requests	Occasionally
		Politeness markers	Rarely to never
	Repairs	Responses to or production of requests	Rarely to never
		Others' corrections or self-repairs to pronunciation, grammar, lexis, pragmatics	Rarely to never

Informal observation	During attempted administration of the *Preschool Language Assessment Instrument,* Travis frequently responded by saying, "Mind your own business." During administration of the *Bracken Basic Concept Scale,* Travis told the examiner, "If you turn the page, you're dead meat." During administration of the *Expressive One-Word Picture Vocabulary Test–Revised,* Travis asked the examiner, "Why do you have underwear on?" (These behaviors could also be descriptive of extralinguistic variables, specifically, inattention to the task.)
	Polite indirect requests (e.g., "Can you show me the _____?") appeared to be taken literally, and Travis responded by saying, "No." When requests were made direct (e.g., "Show me the _____."), Travis did as he was asked.
	Travis was quiet and unresponsive during initial appraisal tasks. Once he warmed up, he occasionally initiated conversation. However, he did not maintain eye contact or effectively participate in turn taking.
Parent interview	See Background Information about Travis in this *Instructor's Supplement* or in the Interview Outcomes in the *CaseFiles* computer program.

[a] errors on lower-case letters and numbers
[b] 85% confidence level
[c] errors on *up* (mastery age: 3;0–3;6), *in back of* (mastery age: 3;6–4;0), *low* (mastery age: 4;6–5;0), and *ahead of* (mastery age: 5;0–5;6)
[d] errors on *we* (mastery age: 4;6–5;0) and *our* (mastery age: 5;0–5;6)

(continued)

RESULTS: TRANSITIONAL LEVEL

Prescbool Language Assessment Instrument

Travis refused to participate in this task.

INTERPRETATION

Semantics

Although Travis's receptive vocabulary skills appear to be below his chronological age by approximately one year, they are within one standard deviation of the mean for children of his age and are considered to be within normal limits. His comprehension of semantic concepts, however, may represent an area of concern. On the *Bracken Basic Concept Scale*, his score fell more than one standard deviation below the mean for children his age and corresponded to an age equivalency that was below his chronological age by approximately one year. His errors on this test were in the areas of letter identification and numbers/counting. While these errors could suggest a conceptual language problem, they could also be related to limited exposure to the concepts. His responses to the semantic concepts sections of the *Vocabulary Comprehension Scale* also suggested possible difficulties with comprehension of conceptual vocabulary. It is important to note, however, that Travis's attention was poor during these tasks, and performances may not be representative of his abilities. Travis's vocabulary production skills, both in terms of lexical entries and vocabulary diversity, appear to be within normal limits for his age.

Morphology and Syntax

Travis demonstrated some difficulty with word forms (pronouns) that should have been mastered by his current age. The syntactic complexity of Travis's expressive language appears to be below age-level expectations. However, the context in which the language sample was obtained may have limited the complexity of Travis's responses. Therefore, these results may not be representative of Travis's linguistic abilities.

Phonology

Travis's phonological production appeared to be age appropriate.

Pragmatics

Among all of the language areas appraised, the pragmatics area was the one that posed the greatest concern. Based upon clinical observation, Travis's pragmatic skills were judged to be inappropriate for a child of any age. His skills were inappropriate for the situation and violated the socially accepted rules for interacting with others.

SPEECH

RESULTS

Informal observation

- Voice characteristics

Voice quality was harsh and hoarse. Characteristics were reported as atypical; mother stated he appeared to be getting a cold.

- Fluency characteristics

Within normal limits

Oral mechanism examination

Travis did not cooperate with efforts to administer an oral peripheral mechanism examination. Informal observation indicated symmetrical external facial structures. During a snack, no drooling was noted and chewing and swallowing functions appeared to be adequate.

(continued)

Appraisal Outcomes: Child-Based Domain—*Continued*	
Parent interview	See Background Information about Travis in this *Instructor's Supplement* or in the Interview Outcomes in the *CaseFiles* computer program.
INTERPRETATION	Travis's speech functions appeared to be grossly within normal limits.

EXTRALINGUISTIC VARIABLES

RESULTS

Informal observation	Upon first meeting Travis in the clinic waiting room, he appeared listless: he walked slowly, as if with great effort, and his body appeared to drag. His listlessness was described as atypical. He had had a DPT shot the day before the appraisal; his mother attributed his behavior to a reaction to the immunization. She was offered the opportunity to bring Travis in on another day when he might be feeling better, but she chose to remain for the appraisal as planned.
	Early in the appraisal session, Travis was quiet and verbally unresponsive. After he "warmed up," he was more verbally responsive, but his responses were often abusive.
	Throughout the evaluation, Travis frequently sat with his head on the table. During pointing tasks, he failed to point to one specific picture; he often pointed to two or more pictures and physically turned away from the examiner and the tasks. On several tasks, most notably the *Preschool Language Assessment Instrument,* Travis flatly refused to do the task at hand. On numerous occasions, he inappropriately flipped pages in test materials and threw various stimulus items around the room. In addition, as noted under pragmatics, Travis demonstrated inappropriate verbal behavior during several appraisal tasks. In general, Travis did not demonstrate focused attention to tasks.
Parent interview	See Background Information about Travis in this *Instructor's Supplement* or in the Interview Outcomes in the *Casefiles* computer program.
INTERPRETATION	Operation of the extralinguistic variables may have influenced Travis's performances in a negative way. His generalized inattention to and limited compliance with appraisal tasks call the accuracy of the language data into question.

APPRAISAL OUTCOMES: SETTING-BASED DOMAIN

COGNITION

Based on information derived from the parent interview, cognitive demands in Travis's home seem congruent with his abilities. His difficulties seem related less to demands placed on him and more to his attentional difficulties as well as his affective responses.

LANGUAGE

Based on information derived from the parent interview, the language demands placed on Travis in his home seem congruent with his developmental level. His problems seem related more to his attentional and pragmatic difficulties than to the demands placed on him in the home environment.

EXTRALINGUISTIC VARIABLES

Based on information derived from the parent interview, efforts are made in the home environment to adapt to Travis's attentional difficulties. These efforts are successful at times, but the parents continue to refine environmental adaptations.

SUGGESTED DISCUSSION ISSUES

Does Travis demonstrate a language disorder?

This question reflects the diagnosis phase of the assessment-intervention process. In addition, it represents one of the major issues that led Travis's parents to seek an evaluation, and students should have an opportunity to address this point in debriefing discussions.

Stated differently, this question might read, "Are Travis's communication performances due to language problems or to inattention/behavior problems?" Although the question is central to Travis's assessment, answering it in definitive terms may not be possible. In that regard, Travis's test results present a confusing picture and call into question the reliability of observed performances. Discrepancies between receptive and expressive abilities, particularly within the semantic area, are difficult to explain on language disorder grounds; the profile presented by Travis's performance is more typically associated with inattention during testing. Moreover, although Travis demonstrates cognitive and language performances that are up to one year delayed compared to his chronological age, his pragmatic performances do not suggest delay per se. Rather, they appear aberrant and would be judged as inappropriate for a child of any age.

From a theory-to-practice perspective, addressing this question also will help students consider the relationship between language comprehension and production. At issue here is whether comprehension skills can be substantially poorer than production. In that regard, debriefing discussion might focus on which theoretical perspectives about language would or would not "allow" such a phenomenon as well as the kinds of interpretations that can be made about the observed behavior under different theories.

An additional theory-to-practice issue raised by this question relates to consideration of the definition of language disorders. Pragmatic disturbances are one of the most common communication problems demonstrated by children with ADHD. Given Travis's history of ADHD and his poor attention throughout the appraisal, a strong possibility exists that his pragmatic problems are related to his ADHD condition. However, at the time of the appraisal, Travis was taking stimulant medication that should have helped him to focus his attention. While we may have seen Travis's best efforts, a more generalized language disorder cannot be entirely ruled out because of the questionable nature of many of his responses to appraisal tasks.

The issue of pragmatics deserves consideration in debriefing discussions because it is difficult to determine if Travis's pragmatic performances reflect a specific disorder in that aspect of language independent of his attention deficit problems. From a theoretical perspective, discussion could focus on how the pragmatics area "fits" with other aspects of language. From a practical point of view, discussion could address whether pragmatic disorders, by themselves, should "qualify" children for intervention.

What predictions can be made about Travis's future language learning and use?

Stated differently, this question addresses how Travis will function in the school setting when he enters kindergarten. As such, it reflects not only the prognosis phase of the assessment-intervention process but also the second major issue that led

Travis's parents to seek an evaluation. It should, therefore, be addressed by students as part of the assessment process during debriefing discussions.

Regardless of whether Travis's problems are language- or attention/behavior-based, a classroom situation will not allow for the performances he demonstrated. Throughout the evaluation, Travis gave clear signals of choice where the situation didn't afford him choice. In a school setting, his responses may be interpreted as a lack of interest or willingness to participate and could be seen as a violation of rules. If Travis engages in this kind of behavior in a school setting, it is unlikely that he will fully benefit from the learning opportunities provided by the environment.

What recommendations should be made for Travis?

Travis's parents were seeking direction in helping their son, and students should focus on the kinds of recommendations to be made on the basis of assessment findings. Given his performances on appraisal tasks, further assessment may be desirable to determine Travis's true cognitive and language abilities and to tease out the contributions of attention and motivation to his performance. Such evaluations could include more naturalistic observation and be extended over a period of time to allow for shorter sessions. In addition, future evaluations could include adaptations and/or selection of procedures that may hold Travis's attention longer.

Debriefing discussions could also focus on issues of demonstrated need versus eligibility. In that regard, Travis might not qualify for services in his local school district, particularly if eligibility criteria

do not allow for pragmatic problems. While addressing this eligibility issue is important, students should be encouraged to move beyond considerations of eligibility and focus on Travis's needs. In that regard, Travis might not need direct, one-to-one speech and language intervention. However, he might benefit from group sessions to focus on developing more appropriate social interaction skills. This kind of counseling could be provided by a speech-language pathologist as part of a language intervention program designed to focus on pragmatic issues. Alternatively, counseling could be provided by a school guidance counselor or a psychologist. An additional possibility might be to focus on social interaction skills within the classroom situation. In that regard, the speech-language pathologist could work collaboratively with the classroom teacher to develop communication groups as part of the language arts curriculum.

Travis's family appears to be aware of the characteristics of ADHD, and they have sought professional help for Travis. However, the family might find it helpful to continue their education about the disorder. In that regard, Travis's family could be referred to Children with Hyperactivity and Attention Deficit Disorder (CHADD), a support group for families of children with ADHD. CHADD is a national group, but many communities have local chapters. In addition, because ADHD presents long-term problems, the family could be encouraged to ongoing counseling for themselves and for Travis. Such counseling can help the family continue to adapt to the changing face of ADHD as Travis gets older. It can also help Travis work with self-concept issues that frequently surface for children with ADHD.

What is the effect of Ritalin and other stimulant medications on children's behaviors?

This question raises issues about the treatment of ADHD that are important for students to understand. Such understanding will help them work with the families of children diagnosed with ADHD as well as with the children themselves.

For children with ADHD who are taking stimulant medication, it is assumed that the medication "solves" attention problems. This assumption is accurate in that stimulant medication helps the child focus his or her attention. However, taking Ritalin for ADHD is not analogous to taking antibiotics for a systemic infection; the medication does not cure the ADHD condition. Moreover, ADHD is a lifelong state, and children require assistance in developing strategies for organizing their behavior and for interacting appropriately in various contexts. In addition, children's families need to understand their role in facilitating the child's development and functioning.

How would students react to Travis's behaviors during the appraisal?

This question raises an important issue that students should consider in the debriefing discussion. Not all children who are seen in clinical settings are adorable and engaging, yet clinicians are obligated to provide appropriate services even if the child is offensive in some way. In that regard, Travis presented a challenge because his behavior and his responses did not invite a positive interaction. In debriefing discussions, students should be encouraged to examine their affective reactions to working with a child like Travis.

What is the relative utility of qualitative versus quantitative methods with Travis?

The actual appraisal plan for Travis included a combination of qualitative and quantitative methods. Moreover, his performances varied on tasks that relied on different methods. Debriefing discussion might address the relative utility of method types. In addition, this question offers opportunities to link theory and practice by considering theoretical positions that might explain differential performance as a function of methodology.

What differences were noticed in students' interview and appraisal plans and those actually implemented in the assessment of Travis?

Students' plans may differ from those actually used in the assessment of Travis. Debriefing on plan differences can help students see that there are numerous ways of approaching assessment of children with suspected language disorders. For example, although the *CaseFiles* computer program offers students the opportunity to plan interviews with Travis's parents and teacher as well as with Travis himself, the actual assessment included only an interview with Travis's mother. If students pursued interviewing Travis and his teacher, debriefing discussions could focus on why these elements were eliminated from the actual assessment as well as the kinds of information that might have been obtained had these interviews been included.

Similarly, in their plans for the setting-based domain, students may have included direct observations of Travis at home and at school. This is a viable appraisal strategy. Although it was not included in the actual appraisal of Travis, students could be encouraged to consider the understanding of Travis and his needs that would have resulted had these observations been conducted as part of the appraisal.

Students should be helped to notice that the actual appraisal plan under the setting-based domain includes specific focus on extralinguistic variables. This target was not routinely included in setting-based plans for the other cases, but it is important to include for Travis. Specifically, discussion might focus on the need for understanding environmental attentional demands placed on Travis as well as the adaptations made for him at home.

LISA

Upper Elementary Language Issues

BACKGROUND INFORMATION

Reason for Referral

An interview with Lisa and her parents was conducted to clarify the family's concerns and to obtain additional information about Lisa. Due to the family's busy schedule, the interview took place in the music department at the Fine Arts Building on the University of Wisconsin-Eau Claire campus so that Lisa's siblings could practice their musical instruments.

Lisa, an 11-year, 8-month-old girl, was referred to the Human Development Center, a multidisciplinery evaluation service, by her parents because of concerns about her academic performance, particularly in math and spelling. Lisa's parents expressed concern about Lisa's educational achievement and her maturity level. They were seeking information about how to assist Lisa toward academic success.

Developmental History

The pregnancy with Lisa was uneventful. However, at the time of delivery, the umbilical cord was wrapped around Lisa's neck. Her parents were unsure whether Lisa received oxygen at that time. Other developmental history was uneventful.

Medical History

Lisa has an extensive medical history related to severe asthma. She was only three weeks old when the asthma began. Since that time, she has had frequent attacks which resulted in three hospitalizations: two weeks when she was eight-and-a-half and twice when she was nine, once for one week and once for five days. Lisa began taking medication for asthma when she was three years old. Because of her asthma, common colds often cause Lisa to be ill for at least a week. Lisa has also had a collapsed lung, and she continues to suffer from allergies. Lisa has recently had her vision checked, and she is waiting for corrective lenses for near vision.

Educational History

Lisa currently is in the sixth grade. She attended the neighborhood public elementary school from kindergarten through fifth grade. For this academic year, Lisa's parents transferred her to St. John's Middle School, a private Catholic school, because they believed that the smaller class size would provide Lisa with greater individualized attention than she had received in the public schools.

Achievement scores from elementary school indicated difficulty in math and spelling. These difficulties have continued into the middle school. Lisa also has illegible handwriting, and she seems unconcerned about the spacing of her writing on the page.

When Lisa has homework, it appears that she is not aware of how to begin the assignment. Once her parents remind her to read the directions and help her with a few problems, she appears to catch on and can continue by herself. However, Lisa constantly requires monitoring from her parents to keep her on task. Additionally, if Lisa has a test the next day, she often does not recognize that she needs to begin studying until it is late at night. Her parents suspect that this may be due to lack of motivation. They believe she wants to do well, but that she may be beginning to get frustrated by her difficulty in some classes.

Lisa has missed approximately three to four weeks of school per year because of asthma attacks and associated hospitalizations. In addition, after nighttime asthma attacks, Lisa's parents let her sleep in the next morning to regain her strength. As a result, she has frequently missed entire mornings of school.

Social, Emotional, and Behavioral History

Lisa is the middle child of three children. She lives with her parents and her siblings in Chippewa Falls, Wisconsin. Her sister is 14 and her brother is 5 years old. Her parents operate a family business.

Due to her asthma, Lisa has always been protected by her parents. They have limited her involvement in sports and social activities out of concern for her health. To compensate, they praise Lisa for the things she can do (e.g., singing). This extra attention has caused tension between Lisa and her older sister who appears jealous of the attention Lisa receives from their parents. She isn't always nice to Lisa, which is apparent to other members of the family.

Lisa's parents have difficulty disciplining her. They believe it is hard to take away her privileges because she is already so limited by her illness. They are lenient with discipline and believe that they should do more. Time-outs are sometimes used with Lisa for disciplining in the moment, but this strategy isn't always successful.

Lisa seems content with unchallenging tasks. When she has friends at her house to play, she often separates and plays by herself on the floor. Her parents believe that this type of behavior is immature for her age. When Lisa was asked about her friends, she only mentioned one friend: Nancy. This year, Lisa began attending a new school. Most of her old friends do not attend this school, and she is trying to make new friends. However, she plays with friends from her old school who still live in her neighborhood.

Lisa appears to have difficulty remembering things such as piano notes, phone numbers, and math facts. Her parents believe that these are things Lisa should remember because she has had repeated exposure to them. Lisa's parents also believe that she may have immature common sense skills. Two examples that they provided were that, even when it's cold out, Lisa will run outside without a coat. They also said she doesn't seem able to color coordinate her clothes. Additional areas of concerns are Lisa's short attention span and difficulty concentrating.

Lisa's illness has contributed to irregular sleeping habits. When she was younger, she awoke every night at approximately 4 a.m. because of asthma attacks which often lasted about an hour. Once the attack was under control, she fell back asleep and her parents let her sleep until she awoke the next morning. She often would not awaken until late morning. During the current school year, her parents have required Lisa to get up every morning in time for school. Because of the irregular pattern in the past, Lisa has not yet caught on to the morning rituals and routines. She continues to need assistance in sequencing the events necessary to get ready for school.

Lisa enjoys arts and crafts activities, playing the guitar, listening to music, and talking on the telephone to her friend, Nancy. Lisa recently became interested in reading for enjoyment. Lisa's parents believe that, compared to other children her age, Lisa is somewhat unconcerned about her appearance.

Speech, Language, and Hearing History

Lisa's speech, language, and hearing development were uneventful and developmental milestones were within normal limits. Lisa's parents did not have specific concerns about her communication skills.

APPRAISAL PLAN AND OUTCOMES

Following is the decision tree broken down visually by domain and target. Following the appraisal decision tree segments are the appraisal outcomes for Lisa.

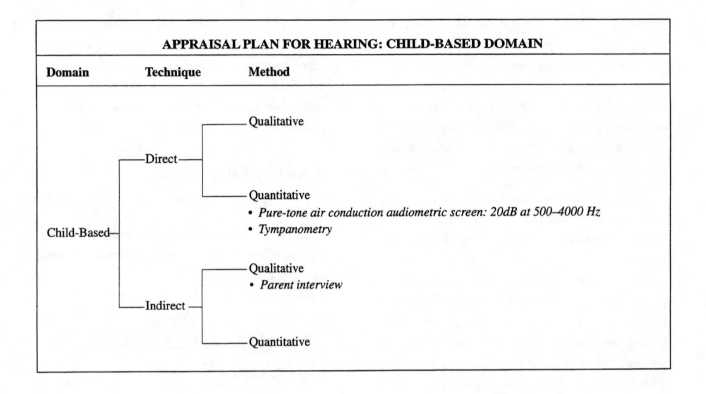

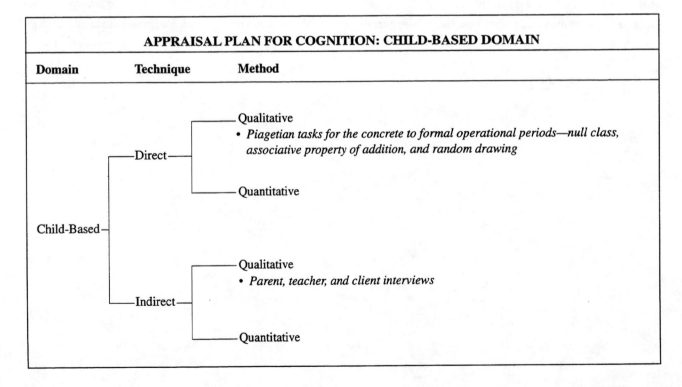

APPRAISAL PLAN FOR LANGUAGE: CHILD-BASED DOMAIN, BASIC LEVEL

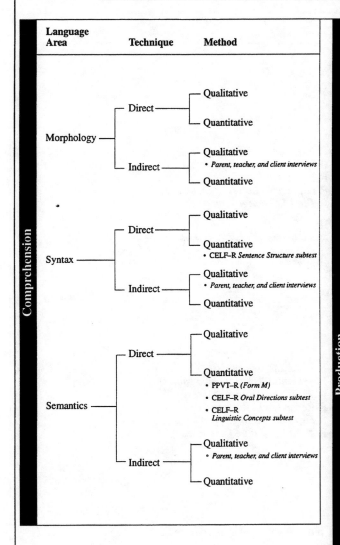

Comprehension

Language Area	Technique	Method

Morphology
- Direct
  - Qualitative
  - Quantitative
- Indirect
  - Qualitative
    - *Parent, teacher, and client interviews*
  - Quantitative

Syntax
- Direct
  - Qualitative
  - Quantitative
    - CELF–R *Sentence Structure subtest*
- Indirect
  - Qualitative
    - *Parent, teacher, and client interviews*
  - Quantitative

Semantics
- Direct
  - Qualitative
  - Quantitative
    - PPVT–R *(Form M)*
    - CELF–R *Oral Directions subtest*
    - CELF–R *Linguistic Concepts subtest*
- Indirect
  - Qualitative
    - *Parent, teacher, and client interviews*
  - Quantitative

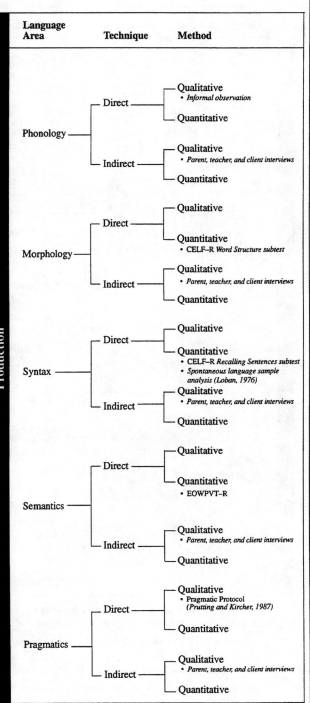

Production

Language Area	Technique	Method

Phonology
- Direct
  - Qualitative
    - *Informal observation*
  - Quantitative
- Indirect
  - Qualitative
    - *Parent, teacher, and client interviews*
  - Quantitative

Morphology
- Direct
  - Qualitative
  - Quantitative
    - CELF–R *Word Structure subtest*
- Indirect
  - Qualitative
    - *Parent, teacher, and client interviews*
  - Quantitative

Syntax
- Direct
  - Qualitative
  - Quantitative
    - CELF–R *Recalling Sentences subtest*
    - *Spontaneous language sample analysis (Loban, 1976)*
- Indirect
  - Qualitative
    - *Parent, teacher, and client interviews*
  - Quantitative

Semantics
- Direct
  - Qualitative
  - Quantitative
    - EOWPVT–R
- Indirect
  - Qualitative
    - *Parent, teacher, and client interviews*
  - Quantitative

Pragmatics
- Direct
  - Qualitative
    - Pragmatic Protocol *(Prutting and Kircher, 1987)*
  - Quantitative
- Indirect
  - Qualitative
    - *Parent, teacher, and client interviews*
  - Quantitative

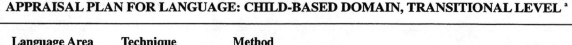

APPRAISAL PLAN FOR LANGUAGE: CHILD-BASED DOMAIN, TRANSITIONAL LEVEL [a]

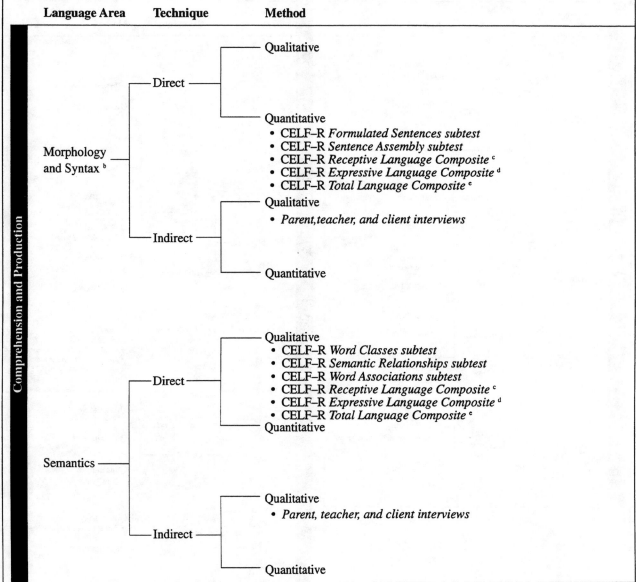

Language Area   **Technique**   **Method**

Comprehension and Production

Morphology and Syntax [b]

Direct — Qualitative

Quantitative
- CELF–R *Formulated Sentences subtest*
- CELF–R *Sentence Assembly subtest*
- CELF–R *Receptive Language Composite* [c]
- CELF–R *Expressive Language Composite* [d]
- CELF–R *Total Language Composite* [e]

Indirect — Qualitative
- *Parent, teacher, and client interviews*

Quantitative

Semantics

Direct — Qualitative
- CELF–R *Word Classes subtest*
- CELF–R *Semantic Relationships subtest*
- CELF–R *Word Associations subtest*
- CELF–R *Receptive Language Composite* [c]
- CELF–R *Expressive Language Composite* [d]
- CELF–R *Total Language Composite* [e]

Quantitative

Indirect — Qualitative
- *Parent, teacher, and client interviews*

Quantitative

[a] At the Transitional Level, most tasks simultaneously demand elements of both comprehension and production or simultaneously demand more complex performances in discrete areas of language.

[b] At the Transitional Level, the language areas of morphology and syntax are frequently represented in a single task, although other areas may be represented discretely.

[c] The Receptive Language Composite Score is derived from scores on the *CELF–R* comprehension subtests.

[d] The Expressive Language Composite Score is derived from scores on the *CELF–R* expression subtests.

[e] The Total Language Composite Score is derived from scores on all *CELF–R* subtests.

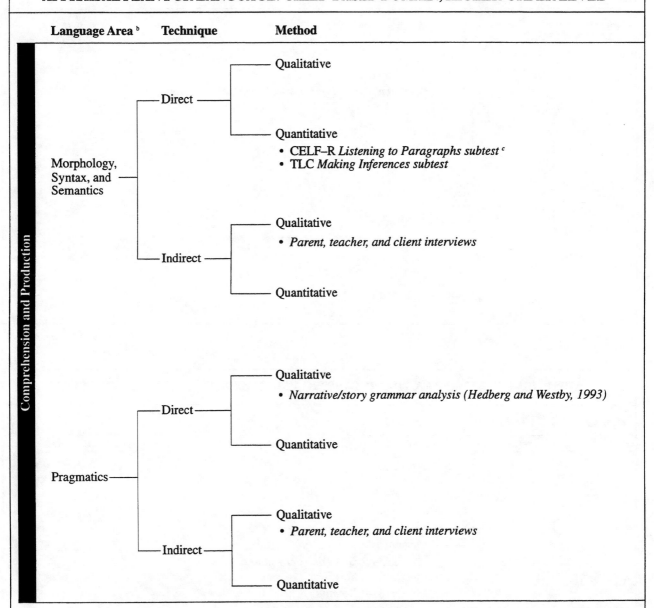

APPRAISAL PLAN FOR LANGUAGE: CHILD-BASED DOMAIN, HIGHER-ORDER LEVEL [a]

Language Area [b]   **Technique**   **Method**

Comprehension and Production

Morphology, Syntax, and Semantics

Direct
- Qualitative
- Quantitative
  - CELF–R *Listening to Paragraphs subtest* [c]
  - TLC *Making Inferences subtest*

Indirect
- Qualitative
  - *Parent, teacher, and client interviews*
- Quantitative

Pragmatics

Direct
- Qualitative
  - *Narrative/story grammar analysis (Hedberg and Westby, 1993)*
- Quantitative

Indirect
- Qualitative
  - *Parent, teacher, and client interviews*
- Quantitative

[a] At the Higher-Order Level, tasks typically are integrated, simultaneously demanding elements of both comprehension and production across all areas of language.

[b] At the Higher-Order Level, all language areas are frequently represented in a single task. However, some tasks are designed and/or selected to allow for specific and different analytic procedures. Thus, the Higher-Order Level portion of the appraisal plan decision tree reflects two distinct branches: the morphology, syntax, and semantics area and the pragmatics area.

[c] Some instructors may take issue with viewing this task as representing the Higher-Order Level. Such differences of perspective and opinion offer rich opportunities for discussion to facilitate critical thinking about appraisal plan specifications and task selection.

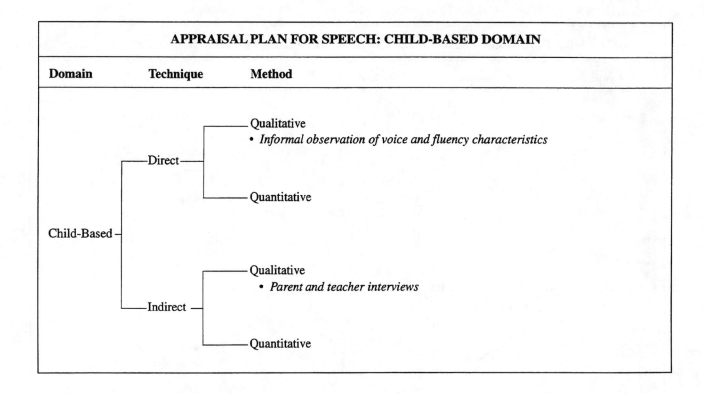

APPRAISAL PLAN FOR SPEECH: CHILD-BASED DOMAIN

Domain	Technique	Method

- Child-Based
  - Direct
    - Qualitative
      - *Informal observation of voice and fluency characteristics*
    - Quantitative
  - Indirect
    - Qualitative
      - *Parent and teacher interviews*
    - Quantitative

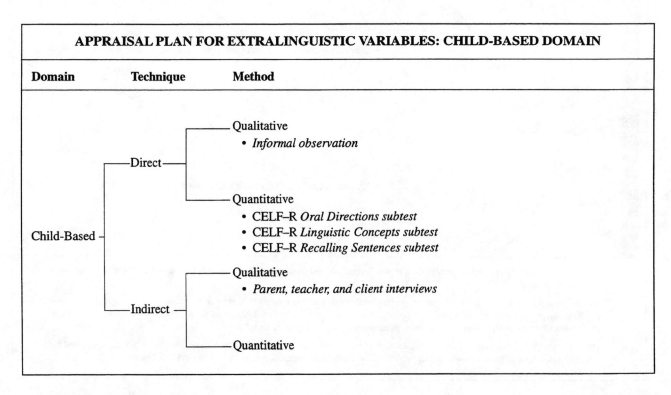

APPRAISAL PLAN FOR EXTRALINGUISTIC VARIABLES: CHILD-BASED DOMAIN

Domain	Technique	Method

- Child-Based
  - Direct
    - Qualitative
      - *Informal observation*
    - Quantitative
      - CELF–R *Oral Directions subtest*
      - CELF–R *Linguistic Concepts subtest*
      - CELF–R *Recalling Sentences subtest*
  - Indirect
    - Qualitative
      - *Parent, teacher, and client interviews*
    - Quantitative

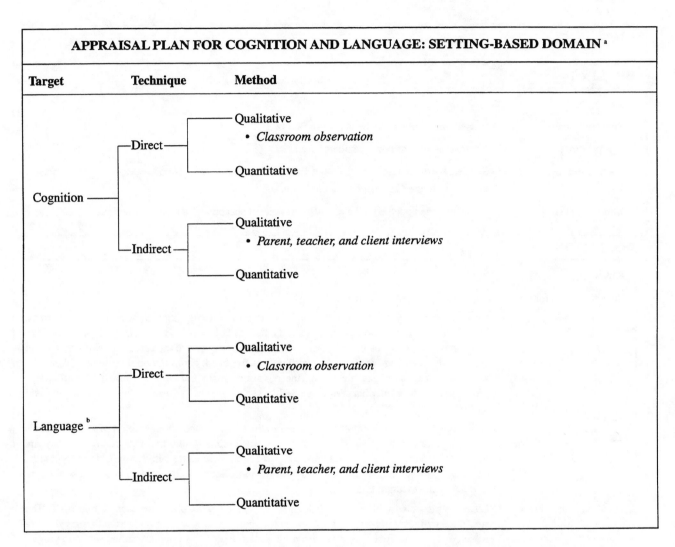

[a] An appraisal plan was determined to be unnecessary for the setting-based domain—hearing, speech, and extralinguistic variables targets.

[b] The language functions of comprehension and production and the language areas of phonology, morphology, syntax, semantics, and pragmatics have been combined in this simple variation of the appraisal decision tree. All three levels of language (basic, transitional, and higher-order) are assumed.

APPRAISAL OUTCOMES: CHILD-BASED DOMAIN

HEARING

RESULTS

Pure-tone screen	Passed bilaterally at 20 dB at 500–4000 Hz
Tympanometry	Normal middle ear pressure bilaterally
Parent interview	See Background Information about Lisa in this *Instructor's Supplement* or in the Interview Outcomes in the *CaseFiles* computer program.
INTERPRETATION	Lisa's hearing appeared to be adequate to support speech and language functions.

COGNITION

RESULTS

Piagetian tasks for the concrete to formal operational periods

- Null class

Lisa was presented with five groups of six cards. The five groups were men, women, trees, houses, and blanks. When asked to classify the cards in any way she chose, Lisa placed the cards into five groups as listed above. When asked to categorize the cards into two groups, she grouped the men and women along with half of the blank cards in one pile; in the other pile, she placed the houses and trees with the remaining blank cards. When asked to explain her groupings, Lisa stated what was contained in each pile (i.e., "These are men and women and half of the plain cards").

Lisa's response is characteristic of children in the concrete operational period of Piaget's levels of intellectual development. Her performance was typical of children between 6 and 10 years of age. She did not realize the blank cards made up a separate set, the null class. Typically, children 10 to 11 years of age can deal with the more abstract notion of a class with something in it and a class with nothing in it.

- Associative property of addition

Lisa was presented with eight cylinders: four cylinders were placed in each of two rows. The first three cylinders in both rows contained the same amount of water. The remaining cylinders were empty. In the first row, water from the first cylinder was poured into the second cylinder of the same row. In the second row, the contents of the second cylinder were combined into the third cylinder. Put in another way, this action would read as: $(A+B) = (B+C)$. Lisa was asked to respond to the question, "If all the cylinders that contain water were poured into the empty cylinders of their respective rows, would one of the cylinders have more, less, or would they be the same?" Put into an equation, this task would read: $(A+B) + C = D; A + (B+C) = D1$, with $D = D1$. Lisa stated that D1 would have more and then changed her answer and said D would contain more. When asked to explain her answer, Lisa provided rationales which were unclear and hard to follow.

Lisa's performance was typical of children between seven and eight years of age. She seemed to remember some of the associations made (e.g., how the liquids were poured). However, she did not realize that the liquids were equal regardless of the order in which they were combined. Typically children between eight and nine years of age use the idea of associative property of addition.

(continued)

Appraisal Outcomes: Child-Based Domain—*Continued*	
• Random drawing	Lisa was presented with two sets of counters, each set consisting of 10 green, 8 red, 6 yellow, and 1 blue. One set of counters was placed in a box while the other set was placed in front of Lisa on the table. Lisa was asked to pick two counters from the box and to predict what colors they would be. On her first pick, Lisa said, "I'll pick green because there are more there." On subsequent picks, she chose the color of the counter she had picked most frequently.
	Initially, Lisa's prediction appeared to take probability into account. However, she did not make adjustments after each trial. This performance indicated that Lisa's understanding of probability is emerging. Most children between the ages of 11 and 12 years have a stable understanding of probability.
Parent, teacher, and client interviews	See Background Information about Lisa in this *Instructor's Supplement* or in the Interview Outcomes in the *CaseFiles* computer program.
INTERPRETATION	Lisa's performances on the Piagetian tasks indicated that she is operating in the concrete operational period (7–10 years). However, limited formal operational skills (11 years+) appear to be emerging. This level of development is grossly within normal limits for Lisa's chronological age.

LANGUAGE

RESULTS: BASIC LEVEL

COMPREHENSION

Semantics

	Raw Score	Standard Score	SEM [a]	Percentile Rank	Age Equivalent
PPVT–R (Form M) (mean standard score = 100, sd = 15)	119	101	6	52	11;11
CELF–R (mean standard score = 10, sd = 3)					
• Oral Directions subtest	17	7	2	16	
• Linguistic Concepts subtest	20	12	2	75	

Parent, teacher, and client interviews	See Background Information about Lisa in this *Instructor's Supplement* or in the Interview Outcomes in the *CaseFiles* computer program.

Morphology

Parent, teacher, and client interviews	See Background Information about Lisa in this *Instructor's Supplement* or in the Interview Outcomes in the *CaseFiles* computer program.

Syntax

	Raw Score	Standard Score	SEM [a]	Percentile Rank	Age Equivalent
CELF–R (mean standard score = 10, sd = 3)					
• Sentence Structure subtest	26	14	1	91	

(continued)

Appraisal Outcomes: Child-Based Domain—*Continued*

| Parent, teacher, and client interviews | See Background Information about Lisa in this *Instructor's Supplement* or in the Interview Outcomes in the *CaseFiles* computer program. |

PRODUCTION

Phonology

| Informal observation | No errors noted |
| Parent, teacher, and client interviews | See Background Information about Lisa in this *Instructor's Supplement* or in the Interview Outcomes in the *CaseFiles* computer program. |

Semantics

	Raw Score	Standard Score	SEM [a]	Percentile Rank	Age Equivalent
EOWPVT–R (mean standard score = 100, sd = 15)	89	117	7.65	87	>11;11

| Parent, teacher, and client interviews | See Background Information about Lisa in this *Instructor's Supplement* or in the Interview Outcomes in the *CaseFiles* computer program. |

Morphology

	Raw Score	Standard Score	SEM [a]	Percentile Rank	Age Equivalent
CELF–R (mean standard score = 10, sd = 3) • Word Structure subtest	35	12	1	75	

| Parent, teacher and client interviews | See Background Information about Lisa in this *Instructor's Supplement* or in the Interview Outcomes in the *CaseFiles* computer program. |

Syntax

	Raw Score	Standard Score	SEM [a]	Percentile Rank	Age Equivalent
CELF–R (mean standard score = 10, sd = 3) • Recalling Sentences subtest	71	12	2	75	

| Spontaneous language sample analysis | Two language samples were collected with Lisa; one was collected during conversation and the other during a narrative construction task. Structural complexity of Lisa's language production was determined from language samples using procedures described by Loban (1976). Analysis yields values for structural complexity: words per communication unit (wds/cu), dependent clauses per communication unit (dc/cu) and fluency (words per maze [wds/maze]), maze words as a percentage of total words (maze %). Values derived from Lisa's samples were compared to values reported by Loban for sixth graders in high, low, and randomly selected reading ability groups. |

(continued)

Appraisal Outcomes: Child-Based Domain—*Continued*

	wds/cu	dc/cu	wds/maze	maze %
• Lisa: conversation	8.74	.30	2.29	4.26
• Lisa: narrative	9.90	.44	2.00	.52
• Loban: high readers	10.32	.41	2.15	6.98
• Loban: low readers	8.57	.30	2.16	10.33
• Loban: randomly selected readers	9.82	.37	2.21	8.29

	Loban's data were derived from narrative samples. Structural complexity values for Lisa's narrative sample correspond to values reported for Loban's randomly selected sixth graders. However, Lisa's conversational sample was less complex. These data suggest that Lisa is capable of using appropriately complex linguistic structures when the situation calls for it. With respect to fluency, Lisa's language use is more fluent (e.g., maze words as a percentage of total words) than her grade-mate peers.
Parent, teacher, and client interviews	See Background Information about Lisa in this *Instructor's Supplement* or in the Interview Outcomes in the *CaseFiles* computer program.

Pragmatics

Pragmatic Protocol (Prutting and Kirchner, 1987)	Lisa's pragmatic skills were appraised informally through observation. Her skills were judged as appropriate for all communicative act dimensions except for vocal intensity; she used a soft voice consistently throughout the appraisal session.
Parent, teacher, and client interviews	See Background Information about Lisa in this *Instructor's Supplement* or in the Interview Outcomes in the *CaseFiles* computer program.

[a] 80% confidence level for the CELF–R Scores

RESULTS: TRANSITIONAL LEVEL

COMPREHENSION AND PRODUCTION

Morphology, Syntax, and Semantics

	Raw Score	Standard Score	SEM [a]	Percentile Rank
CELF–R (mean standard score = 10, sd = 3)				
• Formulated Sentences subtest	52	8	2	25
• Sentence Assembly subtest	14	8	2	25
• Word Classes subtest	23	11	2	63
• Semantic Relationships subtest	23	12	2	75
• Word Associations subtest	41	11	2	63

(continued)

Appraisal Outcomes: Child-Based Domain—*Continued*			
	Raw Score	**SEM** [a]	**Age Equivalent**
CELF–R Composite Scores (mean standard score = 100, sd = 15)			
• Receptive Language Composite	99	7	--
• Expressive Language Composite	95	7	--
• Total Language Composite	97	6	11;1

Parent, teacher, and client interviews	See Background Information about Lisa in this *Instructor's Supplement* or in the Interview Outcomes in the *CaseFiles* computer program.

[a] 80% confidence level for the *CELF–R* Scores

RESULTS: HIGHER-ORDER LEVEL

COMPREHENSION AND PRODUCTION

Morphology, Syntax, and Semantics

	Raw Score	**Standard Score**	**SEM** [a]	**Percentile Rank**
CELF–R (mean standard score = 10, sd = 3)				
• Listening to Paragraphs subtest [b]	7	12	2	75
TLC (mean standard score = 10, sd = 3)				
• Making Inferences subtest	34	13	2	84

Parent, teacher, and client interviews	See Background Information about Lisa in this *Instructor's Supplement* or in the Interview Outcomes in the *CaseFiles* computer program.

Pragmatics

Narrative/story grammar analysis	A narrative sample was collected using the wordless picture book, *Frog on His Own* (Mayer, 1973). Lisa was asked to look through the book and then tell the story using the pictures as a guide. Complexity of Lisa's story grammar structure and her use of cohesion in narrative were analyzed using procedures described by Hedberg and Westby (1993).
• Story grammar analysis	Lisa established a motivating state or a goal for the main character and partially maintained focus on the motive throughout the narrative. However, no episode culminated with an indication of consequences or results of actions related to goals. Motives were not established for other characters in any of the episodes. None of Lisa's episodes were complete or complex; complete and complex episodes are expected to be emerging in students of Lisa's age.
• Cohesion	Lisa's story did not show lapses in cohesion. She used linguistic markers appropriately to tie her discourse together cohesively.
Parent, teacher, and client interviews	See Background Information about Lisa in this *Instructor's Supplement* or in the Interview Outcomes in the *CaseFiles* computer program.

(continued)

Appraisal Outcomes: Child-Based Domain—*Continued*

[a] 80% confidence level for the *CELF–R* scores

[b] Some instructors may take issue with viewing this task as representing the Higher-Order Level. Such differences of perspective and opinion offer rich opportunities for discussion to facilitate critical thinking about appraisal plan specifications and task selection.

INTERPRETATION   In general, Lisa's language testing profile suggests a child with adequate language skills across levels, functions, and areas. Notable exceptions were following semantically meaningful but syntactically unrelated directions and formulating syntactically correct sentences when stimulus words were taken out of context or arranged in ungrammatical strings. These findings were congruent with information derived from various interviews.

SPEECH

RESULTS

Informal observation

- Voice characteristics   Grossly within normal limits; Lisa used an extremely soft voice throughout the appraisal.

- Fluency characteristics   Within normal limits

Parent and teacher interviews   See Background Information about Lisa in this *Instructor's Supplement* or in the Interview Outcomes in the *CaseFiles* computer program.

INTERPRETATION   Lisa's speech functions appeared adequate to support communication functions.

EXTRALINGUISTIC VARIABLES

RESULTS

Informal observation   Lisa was cooperative, and she appeared attentive and motivated during the entire appraisal session.

	Raw Score	Standard Score	SEM[a]	Percentile Rank
CELF–R (mean standard score = 10, sd = 3)				
• Oral Directions subtest [b]	17	7	2	16
• Linguistic Concepts subtest [c]	20	12	2	75
• Recalling Sentences subtest [d]	71	12	2	75

Parent, teacher, and client interviews   See Background Information about Lisa in this *Instructor's Supplement* or in the Interview Outcomes in the *CaseFiles* computer program.

[a] 80% confidence interval

[b] Results of this subtest were interpreted with respect to memory for semantically meaningful but syntactically unrelated material.

[c] Results of this subtest were interpreted with respect to memory for semantically meaningful and syntactically related material.

[d] Results of this subtest were interpreted with respect to memory for syntactically related material.

(continued)

Appraisal Outcomes: Child-Based Domain—*Continued*

INTERPRETATION	Lisa's parents expressed concerns about her memory, and appraisal results may shed light on their concern. Lisa does not seem to demonstrate a generalized memory problem. This conclusion is supported by results from the school psychology evaluation as well as by her performances on the various subtests from the *CELF–R*. On the *WISC–III* Digit Span subtest, a task designed to appraise memory function, Lisa scored at the 50th percentile. On the basis of *CELF–R* results, however, it appears that her memory function is facilitated by a combination of semantic and syntactic meaning. Stimulus items on the Oral Directions subtest rely only on semantic meaning, whereas the other two subtests either specifically involve or imply both semantics and syntax. Given the limited level of inherent meaning in piano notes, telephone numbers, and math facts, it is easier to see why Lisa has difficulties remembering those items.

APPRAISAL OUTCOMES: SETTING-BASED DOMAIN

COGNITION

RESULTS	
Classroom observation	See School Visit Report in *CaseFiles* text.
Parent, teacher, and client interviews	See Background Information about Lisa in this *Instructor's Supplement* or in the Interview Outcomes in the *CaseFiles* computer program.
INTERPRETATION	Cognitive demands placed on Lisa at home and at school are generally congruent with her ability levels. However, expectations within both environments imply greater maturity than Lisa demonstrates. In addition, memory demands in the home and the school setting, although reasonable, are at odds with Lisa's abilities. In that regard, Lisa's difficulties in remembering information that is inherently nonmeaningful interferes with her ability to meet demands in her primary environments.

LANGUAGE

RESULTS	
Classroom observation	See School Visit Report in *CaseFiles* text.
Parent, teacher, and client interviews	See Background Information about Lisa in this *Instructor's Supplement* or in the Interview Outcomes in the *CaseFiles* computer program.
INTERPRETATION	Language demands of both home and school are generally congruent with Lisa's developmental level. However, while acknowledging Lisa's extensive medical history, her family does not see the impact of her illness on her developmental level. In addition, the school environment does not account for affective aspects of Lisa's behavior. In that regard, Lisa's teachers expect students to participate actively in class discussions; such participation is not a behavior that Lisa chooses to engage in. As a result of these features of Lisa's environments, a disparity is noted between her skills and her ability to meet the communicative demands at home and at school.

SUGGESTED DISCUSSION ISSUES

Does Lisa demonstrate a language disorder?

Although Lisa was not referred because of specific language concerns, students should be encouraged to consider the adequacy of her language skills during debriefing discussions. In general, the answer to this question is, probably not. However, her relatively poor performance on several aspects of the language appraisal presents a spiked profile that should be addressed. From a theoretical perspective, considering diagnostic decisions about Lisa will focus students' attention on definitions of language disorder and how they play out in observed performances.

A number of interpretive questions might be raised in debriefing discussions. For example, students should consider how language issues might contribute to Lisa's reported problems. While Lisa may not demonstrate a language disorder per se, students should be helped to interpret her observed performances in light of reported problems. In that regard, the areas in which Lisa shows relatively poorer performances may contribute to the kinds of problems noted in the referral statement. For example, her difficulty remembering items such as phone numbers and math facts could relate to observed memory problems when stimulus items lack inherent meaning.

In addition, discussion could focus on factors in Lisa's background that might contribute to her language profile and reported problems. Searching for cause is not of importance to all language specialists, but in Lisa's case, understanding possible contributors to her current performances may suggest direction for recommendations. Accordingly, students should be encouraged to consider Lisa's performances in light of her history. Of primary concern here is the impact of Lisa's long-term illness on her schooling and her social interactions. Lisa missed an enormous amount of schooling in the elementary years when many basic skills are being established. Missed schooling more recently may have deprived her of opportunities to develop and use metacognitive and metalinguistic strategies and skills. Such a possibility could provide a basis for understanding the areas in which she demonstrates relatively poorer performances.

A related issue is the context within which Lisa's reported problems are perceived. On the basis of all HDC appraisal results, it appears that Lisa is an average to slightly above average child in all areas. Yet her parents' concern led them to seek a comprehensive evaluation. It may be that her parents need reassurance, and students should be encouraged to consider this counseling aspect of the evaluation process. In particular, the parents could be helped to evaluate their expectations of Lisa and to understand the impact on her overall development of her extensive medical history. In addition to these interpretive issues, consideration of possible contributors to Lisa's performance may help students clarify definitions of language disorder and the ways in which language, even in the absence of a disorder, can facilitate or interfere with academic functioning.

What predictions can be made about Lisa's future language learning and use?

It was predicted that Lisa's language skills would continue to expand and that she would succeed in school, continuing to perform at an average to above-average level. These predictions were based on

Lisa's intellectual level, her home and school environments, and the fact that she had recently begun experiencing relatively good health for the first time in her life. While this conclusion was reached by the diagnostic team, debriefing discussions with students might address the predictions they would make as well as the basis for those predictions. Such discussions offer rich opportunities for facilitating students' critical thinking about interpretations of observed assessment performances.

What recommendations should be made for Lisa?

Although Lisa is not a likely candidate for direct language intervention, some adaptive and/or compensatory recommendations can be made to address the problems that led her family to seek an evaluation. Students should be encouraged to consider the kinds of recommendations to be made to Lisa, her family, and her teachers in light of assessment findings. For example, recommendations could be made to help Lisa develop organizational and memory strategies, particularly for material that is inherently nonmeaningful.

Students should also consider recommendations made by other disciplines involved in Lisa's assessment and how those recommendations mesh with each other. For example, the psychology report (see pages 216–218 in the *CaseFiles* text) recommends reducing Lisa's involvement in extracurricular activities so that she has more leisure time. In contrast, the special education report (see pages 219–221 in the *CaseFiles* text) specifically recommends encouraging increased participation in extracurricular activities, particularly in the science area. These recommendations are at odds with each other, and the family may need the opportunity to discuss the disparity as well as ways to reconcile it. In addition, students should

consider recommendations from other disciplines and how those recommendations mesh with suggestions they might offer. For example, the reading report (see pages 222–225 in the *CaseFiles* text) recommends that Lisa be encouraged in "risk taking." It is unclear whether this refers specifically to Lisa's reading activities or to her overall behavioral profile. If the recommendation relates to generalized risk taking, then it is at odds with Lisa's personal style. It may be that Lisa and her family would benefit from reassurances about differences in interactional styles. It might also be recommended that Lisa's teachers acknowledge her style and make demands of her accordingly.

Although it is unlikely that Lisa's performances would qualify her for special education services under Public Law 94-142 and its subsequent amendments, because of her asthma, she is eligible for a Section 504 plan in her school. It might be advisable to recommend that the parents pursue such services if Lisa's problems persist.

What is the relative utility of qualitative versus quantitative methods with Lisa?

For Lisa, this question can highlight important practical and theoretical issues in the use of norm-referenced tests. Much of Lisa's actual appraisal plan is quantitative in nature, and relatively few qualitative procedures were used. This observation provides opportunities for discussion of intelligent use of norm-referenced measures. In addition, the relative utility of norm- and criterion-referenced measures as well as informal procedures and observation might be addressed in debriefing discussions.

A related issue raised by this question is the critical use of normative data; also, interpretations about the structural complexity of Lisa's spontaneous language provide a rich opportunity for discussion of this issue. The language sampling done with Lisa involved collection of both narrative and conversational samples, and Loban's (1976) strategy was used for analysis. It was found that the complexity reflected in Lisa's narrative sample was commensurate with performances of randomly selected readers in her grade, while the complexity reflected in her conversational sample was commensurate with performances of poor readers in her grade. As a preliminary discussion point, students should consider whether these findings are contradictory. Moving to a broader level of interpretation, it is important to note that Loban's data were derived from narrative samples. At issue here is whether Loban's data can be used with conversational samples. If so, how? If not, why not? Linking these theoretical and interpretive issues to practice, students might also be helped to consider the kinds of language samples they choose to collect during appraisals and the ways in which normative data can be applied to various samples.

In what ways is the planning framework different at various language levels?

As can be seen from the Appraisal Plan that was presented for Lisa previously in this *Instructor's Supplement,* the decision tree is structured differently at the basic, transitional, and higher-order levels of language. This may be confusing for some students who may want to address the components of language discretely at all times. The most obvious discussion

point here is the theory-to-practice issue of how language works at different levels of demand. Particularly in assessments with older elementary-age children and adolescents, appraisal needs to move beyond the basic level. Students should be helped to see the conceptual difficulty in thinking about language areas as discrete elements at transitional and higher-order levels.

What is the relative utility of indirect versus direct techniques?

Visual inspection of the appraisal planning decision tree for Lisa, and for the other cases as well, shows that the indirect techniques branch is frequently bare. On its face, this observation focuses on issues of task selection. However, it also offers opportunities to discuss the appropriateness, adequacy, validity, and reliability of indirect versus direct techniques and measures.

What differences were noted in students' interview and appraisal plans and those actually implemented in the assessment of Lisa?

Students' plans may differ from those actually used in the assessment of Lisa. For example, students may have decided to use more qualitative methods than were used in the actual appraisal. Debriefing on these differences can help students see that there are numerous ways of approaching assessment of children with suspected language disorders.

ADAM
Adolescent Language Issues

BACKGROUND INFORMATION

Adam was evaluated by students and staff members of the Human Development Center (HDC), which operates a multidisciplinary, psychoeducational evaluation team. An interview was conducted with Adam and his mother by graduate students in communication disorders and school psychology. The purpose of the interview was to clarify information and concerns about Adam's poor school performance.

Identification and Statement of the Problem

Adam is a 14-year, 10-month-old male. Adam lives with his mother, his older brother, and his younger sister; his father is deceased. Adam attends Sacred Heart Senior High School in the 9th grade. Adam's mother hopes to discover some learning strategies for Adam that will help him learn, concentrate, and comprehend better. She believes he is intelligent but needs a different way to learn compared to other children.

General Development

Pregnancy and Delivery

The pregnancy with Adam was uneventful. Adam's mother had a cesarean section for the birth of her older son; Adam was delivered through a repeat cesarean section. Adam's mother had an epidural anesthetic for Adam's birth. She had the epidural procedure done previously with no complication, but for Adam's delivery the spinal "went wrong." The needle was inserted too far into the meninges of the spinal cord, and the medication numbed the upper half of her body so she could not feel her arms and had difficulty breathing. The delivery itself was uneventful, but Adam's mother experienced amnesia for a short time after the delivery and had spinal headaches for two years after Adam's birth.

Early Development

Adam was described as a good baby, but he was passive, lethargic, and sleepy. Because Adam slept a lot, and because his mother was still in pain and on medication from her spinal, the doctor recommended not waking Adam to breast-feed him. Once, three days went by before Adam woke for a feeding. Adam was a small and fragile baby with poor muscle tone. At one month, his mother held Adam so he could stand on the table, but she noticed that he did not push on the table with his foot as his older brother had done. Adam was taken to the doctor, but the doctor showed no concern. When Adam was three months old, his family moved, and had a new doctor. That doctor was worried about Adam's motor development, but blood tests revealed that Adam was normal. The doctor decided he was developing slowly motorically and gave Adam's parents exercises to strengthen his legs. His mother expressed concern that, at the time Adam was learning to walk, he frequently pulled himself up by the windowsill and teethed on it. This did not concern Adam's mother at the time, but now she has heard reports of lead in the paint of extremely old houses. Their house is over 100 years old. At the time, there were no tests done on the paint or on Adam so it is unclear if the paint had lead in it or if Adam was affected. Adam's mother had no other concerns about Adam's early development. He talked early and was easy to understand so she has never had concerns about Adam's speech and language development.

Medical History

Adam is and has always been healthy. No major hospitalizations or illnesses were noted. At Adam's prekindergarten screening, a ticking watch was held up to his ear, and he could not hear the ticking. Adam had wax build-up in his ear, and he frequently had warm ear washes to remove the wax. His mother thought that the wax could have affected Adam's hearing. However, he reacted the same to her requests and commands both before and after ear washes.

Adam does not wear glasses and has passed all the vision screenings for school.

Educational Information

Views of School Personnel

Starting in kindergarten, Adam's teachers described him as having low concentration. Adam had a particularly hard year in second grade. His teacher belittled him and called him a poor reader. She told Adam's mother that he was a discipline problem and a talker. When Adam read in front of the class, he experienced difficulty. Adam's mother went to school many times that year to defend her son. She asked the teacher if Adam could bring home his readers to prepare for oral reading, and the teacher agreed for a short time. When his mother helped him, Adam seemed to understand better. But the teacher stopped letting Adam bring home the readers, so he was still frustrated with his reading. Adam's mother believed that the second grade teacher suppressed Adam's self-concept.

In third grade, Adam transferred to the public schools. His teacher reported that Adam had a problem with self-esteem and that he could not read. Adam was good with numbers at that time, so the teacher tried to boost his self-confidence by announcing that Adam got good grades on math assignments. The third grade was a year of building up Adam's self-concept.

Adam's mother met with his ninth grade teachers and asked that Adam be treated like he had a learning disability until proved otherwise. All the teachers agreed, but Adam's Western Civilization teacher was reluctant.

Course Work

In the first semester of ninth grade, Adam failed most of his classes. He described Western Civilization, physical science, and English as "hard." In Western Civilization, students outline chapters, complete map assignments, and take tests. The tests consist of essays and vocabulary words. Adam prepares for exams by studying last year's tests and reading the textbook to look for potential essay questions. The vocabulary segment is easier than the essay segment. Science involves knowing formulas and knowing what numbers to insert into them. Adam doesn't believe it is necessary to read the textbook because the instructor always puts the key points from the chapters on an overhead. Even though this class involves numbers, which are Adam's strength, he does not understand how to put them into the formulas. Adam's English class just finished a speech unit. Adam enjoyed this unit, and he did well in it. Adam did speeches on snowboarding, capital punishment, and how he gets ready for school in the morning. Currently, the class is reading *Huckleberry Finn* by Mark Twain. Adam finds the reading boring, and he does not enjoy it. Adam's mother later explained that Adam finds it difficult and refuses help from her. Adam recently had a comprehension test on the book; he got 4 of 26 questions correct.

Study Habits

Adam described his study habits as "decent." His friends never have homework, but he has approximately 30 minutes of homework every night. He rarely studies with his friends but sometimes studies with his brother for Western Civilization. Adam's mother did not agree that Adam's study habits were decent. He studies in the living room with the television on. After supper, everyone is to study for 30 minutes; if they have no homework, they are supposed to find a book to read. This technique no longer works; Adam sits at the kitchen table and spins his pencil to avoid studying. His concentration has always been poor, and he procrastinates doing his homework until after nine o'clock. He lets talking to his friends interrupt his studies. His mother sees Adam doing work for algebra and Western Civilization at home but not for other courses. The school offers a special time in the morning before school for students who want or need special help. Adam went for a couple of months last semester, but he rarely goes now. He described it as a study hall. If someone has questions about any class but algebra, they can ask the teacher, but there is no group work or individualized attention. Adam said that it is not very helpful. He usually finishes his homework from the night before.

Reading

Adam likes to read anything about snowboarding or things that interest him. *Huckleberry Finn* is boring and slow reading, but he understands it. Western Civilization is easy to read, and he can get the facts by reading a chapter a couple of times. Adam's mother reported that Adam has always had problems reading, and the problem seems to have gotten worse as Adam has gotten older.

Social, Emotional, and Behavioral History

Parental Occupation

Adam's mother is a nurse and alternates between day and night shifts. She is available to pick the children up from school and to get Adam to wrestling practice. Adam's father passed away when Adam was 10 years old. No mention was made of his employment or how much time he spent with the family.

Siblings

Adam's older brother, James, is 16 years old. James has always done well in school. James knows he does better schoolwork and often irritates Adam with that knowledge. Adam's sister, Amy, is nine years old and is in the gifted and talented program at her school. Adam's mother believes it is hard for Adam to be the middle child between two siblings who excel in school.

Family Activities

The family watches television together. Their favorite place to go out to eat together is the Country Buffet. The whole family also usually goes to the open skating session at the local ice arena on Sundays.

Discipline

Grounding the children is an effective means of discipline. Adam values his social life, and, if that is taken away, he realizes the seriousness of his actions. In the past, Adam's mother has grounded both Adam and James and required that their free time be spent with her and Amy. Sometimes the grounding is harder on her than it is on the boys, but if she makes a disciplinary threat, she will not back down from it. During the year-and-a-half after his father died, Adam was extremely angry and rebellious, and no disciplinary technique worked. In that time period, being grounded meant nothing to Adam. It was not until later that he learned how valuable his social time with his friends was.

Social Life

Adam is very social, has lots of friends, and gets along well with all of his teachers and the adults in his life. Adam enjoys snowboarding with his friends. He also likes to go ice fishing and to hang out with his friends at the mall or anywhere but at home. In the summer, Adam likes to Roller Blade, play baseball, fish, and swim with his friends.

Emotional Behaviors

Adam's mother described Adam as having a quick temper. The easiest way to set him off is to call him "stupid." That makes him mad enough to go after someone with his fists, most often his brother, James. Often his anger will be displayed through yelling and screaming. After Adam displays his temper, he goes off alone to pout. Adam does not show anger toward school or his teachers and never displays this violent temper at school. Adam had a lot of anger and was very rebellious after his father died. Adam was so hard to handle that his mother considered putting him in a foster home. Even though the year-and-a-half after his father's death was an unstable time for everyone in the family, it was Adam who comforted his mother in her weak moments by saying, "I love you" or "Don't cry, Mom." The family still has hard times dealing with the death of their father. Adam's mother described Adam as a very impressionable boy. He is embarrassed and afraid about the HDC evaluation and sometimes cries at the thought that he is "mental."

APPRAISAL PLAN AND OUTCOMES

Following is an appraisal decision tree broken down visually by domain and target. Following the appraisal decision tree segments are the appraisal outcomes for Adam.

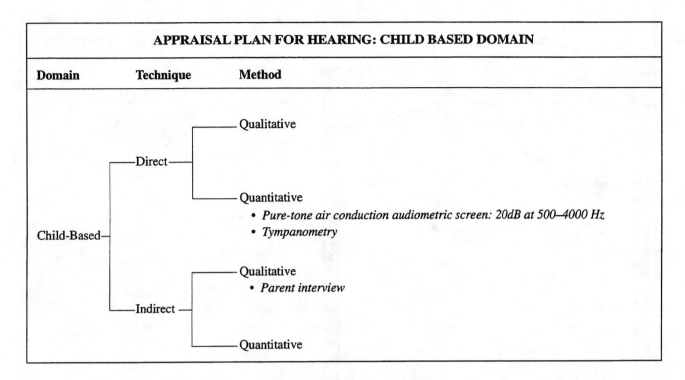

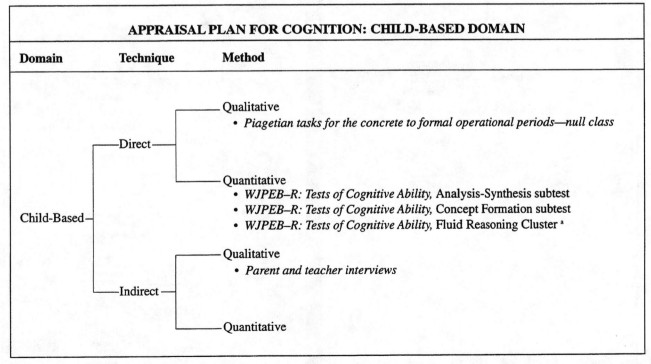

[a] This cluster score is derived from scores on the Analysis-Synthesis and Concept Formation subtests. Fluid Reasoning is conceptualized as the capability to reason in novel situations.

APPRAISAL PLAN FOR LANGUAGE: CHILD-BASED DOMAIN, BASIC LEVEL

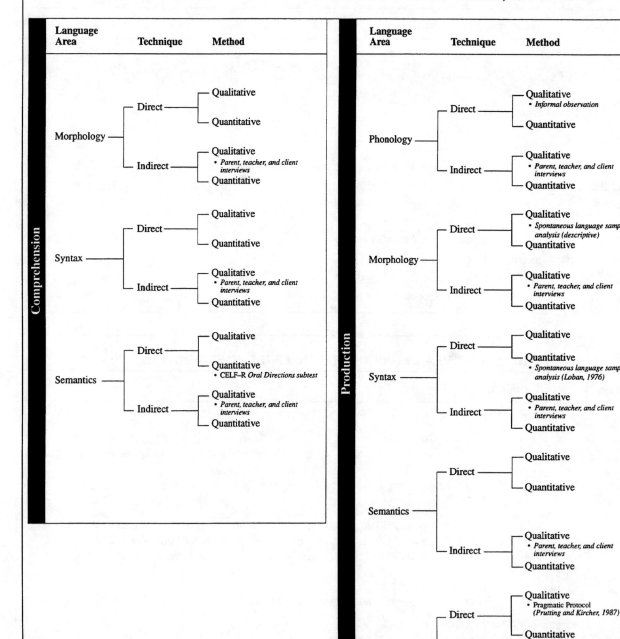

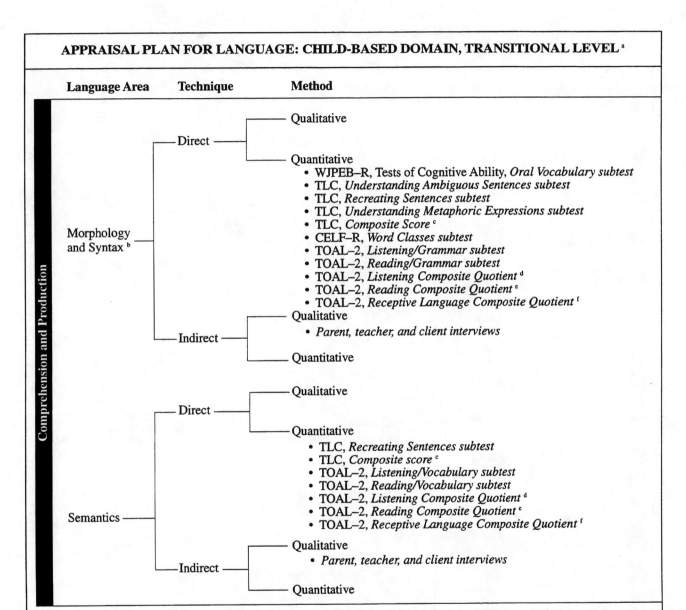

APPRAISAL PLAN FOR LANGUAGE: CHILD-BASED DOMAIN, TRANSITIONAL LEVEL [a]

Language Area	Technique	Method

Comprehension and Production

Morphology and Syntax [b]

Direct — Qualitative

— Quantitative
- WJPEB–R, Tests of Cognitive Ability, *Oral Vocabulary subtest*
- TLC, *Understanding Ambiguous Sentences subtest*
- TLC, *Recreating Sentences subtest*
- TLC, *Understanding Metaphoric Expressions subtest*
- TLC, *Composite Score* [c]
- CELF–R, *Word Classes subtest*
- TOAL–2, *Listening/Grammar subtest*
- TOAL–2, *Reading/Grammar subtest*
- TOAL–2, *Listening Composite Quotient* [d]
- TOAL–2, *Reading Composite Quotient* [e]
- TOAL–2, *Receptive Language Composite Quotient* [f]

Indirect — Qualitative
- *Parent, teacher, and client interviews*

— Quantitative

Semantics

Direct — Qualitative

— Quantitative
- TLC, *Recreating Sentences subtest*
- TLC, *Composite score* [c]
- TOAL–2, *Listening/Vocabulary subtest*
- TOAL–2, *Reading/Vocabulary subtest*
- TOAL–2, *Listening Composite Quotient* [d]
- TOAL–2, *Reading Composite Quotient* [e]
- TOAL–2, *Receptive Language Composite Quotient* [f]

Indirect — Qualitative
- *Parent, teacher, and client interviews*

— Quantitative

[a] At the Transitional Level, most tasks simultaneously demand elements of both comprehension and production or simultaneously demand more complex performances in discrete areas of language.

[b] At the Transitional Level, the language areas of morphology and syntax are frequently represented in a single task, although other areas may be represented discretely.

[c] The Composite Score on the *TLC* is derived from the sum of the raw scores for the Understanding Ambiguous Sentences, Understanding Metaphoric Expressions, and Making Inferences subtests. (See Higher-Order Level Appraisal Plan for performances on Making Inferences subtest.)

[d] The Listening Composite Quotient on the *TOAL–2* is derived from the sum of the standard scores for the Listening/Vocabulary and Listening/Grammar subtests.

[e] The Reading Composite Quotient on the *TOAL–2* is derived from the sum of the standard scores for the Reading/Vocabulary and Reading/Grammar subtests.

[f] The Receptive Language Composite Quotient on the *TOAL-2* is derived from the sum of the standard scores for the Listening/Vocabulary, Listening/Grammar, Reading/Vocabulary, and Reading/Grammar subtests.

APPRAISAL PLAN FOR LANGUAGE: CHILD-BASED DOMAIN, HIGHER-ORDER LEVEL [a]

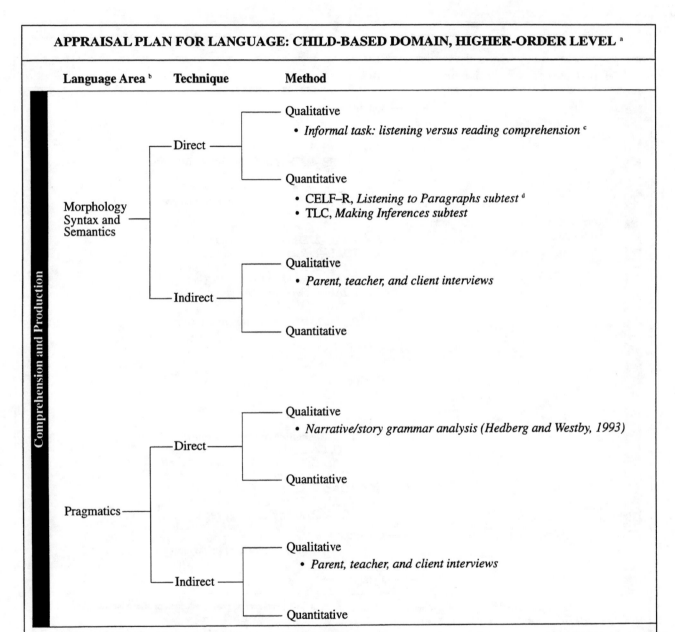

[a] At the Higher-Order Level, tasks typically are integrated, simultaneously demanding elements of both comprehension and production across all areas of language.

[b] At the Higher-Order Level, all language areas are frequently represented in a single task. However, some tasks are designed and/or selected to allow for specific and different analytic procedures. Thus, the Higher-Order Level appraisal plan decision tree reflects two distinct branches: the morphology, syntax, and semantics areas and the pragmatics area.

[c] Paragraphs from the *CELF–R* Listening to Paragraphs subtest were used informally to compare Adam's ability to comprehend material read aloud to him with his comprehension of material he read silently. For each paragraph, he was asked both factual and inferential questions.

[d] Some instructors may take issue with viewing this task as representing the Higher-Order Level. Such differences of perspective and opinion offer rich opportunities for discussion to facilitate critical thinking about appraisal plan specifications and task selection.

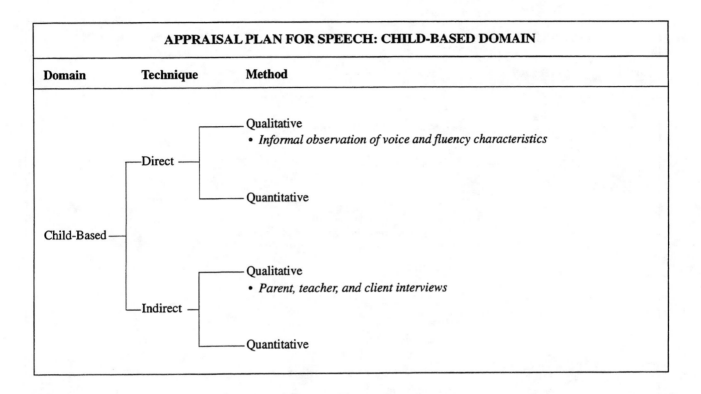

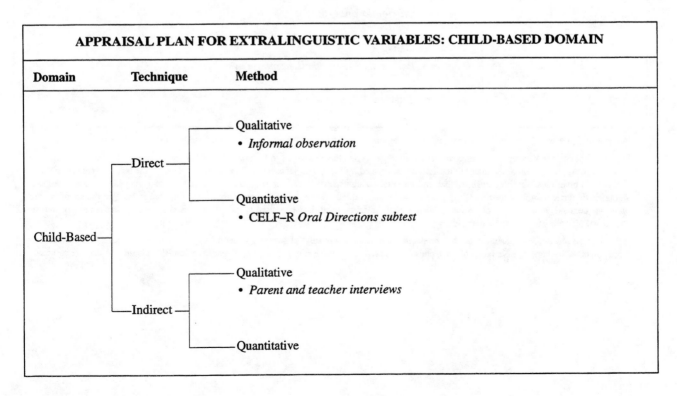

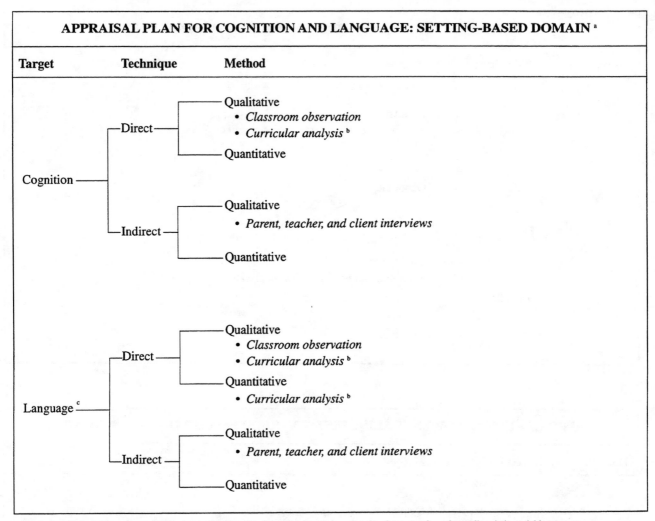

APPRAISAL PLAN FOR COGNITION AND LANGUAGE: SETTING-BASED DOMAIN [a]

Target	Technique	Method

Cognition
— Direct — Qualitative
  • *Classroom observation*
  • *Curricular analysis* [b]
  — Quantitative
— Indirect — Qualitative
  • *Parent, teacher, and client interviews*
  — Quantitative

Language [c]
— Direct — Qualitative
  • *Classroom observation*
  • *Curricular analysis* [b]
  — Quantitative
  • *Curricular analysis* [b]
— Indirect — Qualitative
  • *Parent, teacher, and client interviews*
  — Quantitative

[a] An appraisal plan was determined to be unnecessary for the setting-based domain—hearing, speech, and extralinguistic variables targets.

[b] Adam's textbook for Western Civilization was analyzed to determine the cognitive and language demands inherent in that document. Information provided in Appraisal Outcomes relates to the analysis performed by the speech-language assessment team. Because the text analyzed may not be available in other locations, it is suggested that students obtain a high school-level textbook and use strategies for analyzing cognitive and language demands in curriculum described by Cirrin (1994) and Gruenewald and Pollak (1990). If students are not required to analyze the cognitive and language demands in a high school text, data derived from the actual analysis can be used in interpreting the cognitive and language demands on Adam and his ability to meet those demands.

[c] The language functions of comprehension and production and the language areas of phonology, morphology, syntax, semantics, and pragmatics have been combined in this simple variation of the appraisal decision tree. All three levels of language (basic, transitional, and higher-order) are assumed.

APPRAISAL OUTCOMES: CHILD-BASED DOMAIN

HEARING

RESULTS

Pure-tone screening	Passed bilaterally at 20 dB at 500–4000 Hz
Tympanometry	Normal middle ear pressure bilaterally
Parent interview	See Background Information about Adam in this *Instructor's Supplement* or in the Interview Outcomes in the *CaseFiles* computer program.
INTERPRETATION	Adam's hearing appeared to be adequate to support speech and language functions.

COGNITION

RESULTS

Piagetian task for the concrete to formal operational periods

- Null class

Adam was given four groups of cards with six cards in each group. The four groups were foods, transportation, animals, and blanks. When asked to classify the cards in any way he chose, Adam placed the cards into four groups as listed above. When asked to categorize the cards into two groups, he placed the blank cards in one group and cards with pictures on them in another group. Adam then stated that one set of cards had pictures on them, and the other set was blank.

Adam's performance is characteristic of students in the Formal Operational period (age 11 and older). He dealt with the abstract notion of a class with nothing in it, the null class.

	Raw Score	SS	SEM	%ile Rank	Age	Grade	RMI
WJPEB–R,							
Tests of Cognitive Ability							
• Analysis-Synthesis subtest	24	94	6	34	11;10	6.6	81/90 [a]
• Concept Formation subtest	28	103	4	59	19;0	11.8	93/90 [b]
• Fluid Reasoning Cluster		99	4	48	13;10	9.1	89/90 [c]

Parent and teacher interviews	See Background Information about Adam in this *Instructor's Supplement* or in the Interview Outcomes in the *CaseFiles* computer program.

[a] The Relative Mastery Index means that Adam would be expected to demonstrate 81% mastery with similar tasks that average individuals in his age group would perform with 90% mastery.

[b] The Relative Mastery Index means that Adam would be expected to demonstrate 93% mastery with similar tasks that average individuals in his age group would perform with 90% mastery.

[c] The Relative Mastery Index means that Adam would be expected to demonstrate 89% mastery with similar tasks that average individuals in his age group would perform with 90% mastery.

(continued)

| INTERPRETATION | Adam's performances on the various cognitive tasks suggest adequate ability to problem solve under both relatively language-free and relatively language-bound conditions. This finding supports, and is supported by, Adam's mother's belief that he is intelligent but may need a different way to learn. |

LANGUAGE

RESULTS: BASIC LEVEL

COMPREHENSION

Morphology

| Parent, teacher, and client interviews | See Background Information about Adam in this *Instructor's Supplement* or in the Interview Outcomes in the *CaseFiles* computer program. |

Syntax

| Parent, teacher, and client interviews | See Background Information about Adam in this *Instructor's Supplement* or in the Interview Outcomes in the *CaseFiles* computer program. |

Semantics

	Raw Score	Standard Score	SEM [a]	Percentile Rank
CELF–R Oral Directions subtest mean standard score = 10, sd = 3)	21	11	2	63

| Parent, teacher, and client interviews | See Background Information about Adam in this *Instructor's Supplement* or in the Interview Outcomes in the *CaseFiles* computer program. |

PRODUCTION

Phonology

| Informal observation | No errors noted. |

| Parent, teacher, and client interviews | See Background Information about Adam in this *Instructor's Supplement* or in the Interview Outcomes in the *CaseFiles* computer program. |

Morphology and Syntax

| Spontaneous language sample analysis | Spontaneous language samples were collected during conversation with Adam and during two narrative construction tasks. Structural complexity of Adam's language production was determined from the three language samples using procedures described by Loban (1976). Analysis yields values for structural complexity: words per communication unit (wds/cu), dependent clauses per communication unit (dc/cu) and fluency (words per maze [wds/maze]), maze |

(continued)

words as a percentage of total words (maze %). Values derived from Adam's samples were compared to values reported by Loban for ninth graders in high, low, and randomly selected reading ability groups.

	wds/cu	**dc/cu**	**wds/maze**	**maze %**
• Adam: conversation	7.68	.20	2.00	1.32
• Adam: narrative tell	11.48	.52	—	—
• Adam: narrative retell	12.09	.50	—	—
• Loban: high readers	11.73	.52	1.78	5.31
• Loban: low readers	9.26	.31	2.18	10.18
• Loban: randomly selected readers	10.95	.43	11.98	7.29

Loban's data were derived from narrative samples. Structural complexity values for Adam's narrative samples correspond to values reported for Loban's ninth graders from the high reading group. However, Adam's conversational sample was less complex. These data suggest that Adam is capable of using appropriately complex linguistic structures when the situation calls for it. With respect to fluency, Adam's language use under narrative conditions is more fluent (e.g., maze words as a percentage of total words) than his grade-mate peers. Under conversational conditions, Adam's fluency in terms of words per maze is more like the fluency shown by Loban's low reading group. However, in terms of maze words as a percentage of total words, Adam's conversational language is more fluent than his grade-mate peers.

Parent, teacher, and client interviews	See Background Information about Adam in this *Instructor's Supplement* or in the Interview Outcomes in the *CaseFiles* computer program.

Semantics

Parent, teacher, and client interviews	See Background Information about Adam in this *Instructor's Supplement* or in the Interview Outcomes in the *CaseFiles* computer program.

Pragmatics

Pragmatic Protocol	Adam's pragmatic skills were appraised informally through observation. His skills were judged as appropriate for all communicative act dimensions.
Parent, teacher, and client interviews	See Background Information about Adam in this *Instructor's Supplement* or in the Interview Outcomes in the CaseFiles computer program.

[a] 80% confidence level

(continued)

Appraisal Outcomes: Child-Based Domain—*Continued*

RESULTS: TRANSITIONAL LEVEL

COMPREHENSION AND PRODUCTION

Morphology, Syntax, and Semantics

	Raw Score	SS	SEM	%ile Rank	Age	Grade	RMI
WJPEB–R, *Tests of Cognitive Ability* (mean standard score = 100, sd = 15) • Oral Vocabulary subtest	24	94	5	33	12;10	7.4	77/90 [a]

	Raw Score	Standard Score	SEM [b]	Percentile Rank	Age Equivalent
TLC (Individual subtests mean standard score = 10, sd = 3)					
• Understanding Ambiguous Sentences subtest	35	13	2	84	
• Recreating Sentences subtest	71	10	2	50	
• Understanding Metaphoric Expressions subtest	25	9	2	37	
Composite Score [c] (mean = 100, sd = 15)	161	99	2	47	14;3

	Raw Score	Standard Score	SEM [b]	Percentile Rank
CELF–R (mean standard score =10, sd = 3) • Word Classes subtest	26	14	2	91

	Raw Score	Standard Score	SEM [b]	Percentile Rank	Age Equivalent
TOAL-2 (Individual subtests, mean standard score = 10, sd = 3)					
• Listening/ Vocabulary subtest	22	11	1	63	
• Listening/ Grammar subtest	13	6	1	9	

(continued)

Appraisal Outcomes: Child-Based Domain—*Continued*

	Raw Score	Standard Score	SEM [b]	Percentile Rank	Age Equivalent
• Reading/ Vocabulary subtest	26	12	1	75	
• Reading/ Grammar subtest	13	7	1	16	
Composites (mean standard score = 100, sd = 50)					
• Listening Composite [d]		17	3		91
• Reading Composite [e]		19	3		97
• Receptive Language Composite [f]		36	3		93

Parent, teacher, and client interviews	See Background Information about Adam in this *Instructor's Supplement* or in the Interview Outcomes in the *CaseFiles* computer program.

[a] The Relative Mastery Index means that Adam would be expected to demonstrate 77% mastery with similar tasks that average individuals in his age group would perform with 90% mastery.

[b] 80% confidence interval

[c] Composite values were derived from the sum of the raw scores for the Understanding Ambiguous Sentences, Recreating Sentences, Understanding Metaphoric Expressions, and Making Inferences subtests. See Higher Order tasks for performances on Making Inferences subtest.

[d] The Listening Composite value was derived from the sum of the standard scores for the Listening/Vocabulary and Listening/Grammar subtests.

[e] The Reading Composite value was derived from the sum of the standard scores for the Reading/Vocabulary and Reading/Grammar subtests.

[f] The Receptive Language Composite value was derived from the sum of the standard scores for the Listening/Vocabulary, Listening/Grammar, Reading/Vocabulary and Reading/Grammar subtests.

RESULTS: HIGHER-ORDER LEVEL

COMPREHENSION AND PRODUCTION

Morphology, Syntax, Semantics, and Pragmatics

	Raw Score	Standard Score	SEM [a]	Percentile Rank
CELF–R, (mean standard score = 10, sd = 3) • Listening to Paragraphs subtest [b]	5	9	3	37
TLC (mean standard score = 10, sd = 3) • Making Inferences subtest	30	8	3	25

(continued)

Appraisal Outcomes: Child-Based Domain—*Continued*

Informal task: listening versus reading comprehension	Paragraphs from the *CELF–R* Listening to Paragraphs subtest were used informally to compare Adam's ability to comprehend material read aloud to him with his comprehension of material he read silently. For each paragraph, he was asked both factual and inferential questions.			
	Listening to Paragraphs		Reading Paragraphs	
	Factual Questions	Inferential Questions	Factual Questions	Inferential Questions
	2/4 correct	2/2 correct	3/4 correct	1/2 correct

Narrative/story grammar analysis	Two narrative samples were collected using the wordless picture book, *Frog on His Own* (Mayer, 1973). Adam was asked to look through the book and then tell the story using the pictures as a guide. This was designated the "tell" condition. He was then asked to retell the story without the pictures. This was designated the "retell" condition. Complexity of Adam's story grammar structure and his use of cohesion in narrative was analyzed using procedures described by Hedberg and Westby (1993). In addition, Adam's use of cohesive devices was also analyzed in his conversational sample.
• Story grammar structure	Adam established a motivating state or a goal for the main character, and he maintained focus on the motive throughout the narrative. He also established motives for other characters in several of the episodes. However, no episode culminated with an indication of consequences or results of actions related to goals. None of Adam's episodes were complete or complex; complete and complex episodes are expected of students Adam's age. Furthermore, the complexity of Adam's story was the same on the "tell" and the "retell" conditions; Adam basically told the same story under both conditions. Students' stories frequently increase in complexity from the "tell" to the "retell" condition. Lacking the book to structure the story's elements, the student is forced to filter the narration through his or her own story grammar structure organizational system. Such story grammar structure knowledge is viewed as contributory to recall and comprehension of text.
• Cohesion	Adam's story did not show lapses in cohesion; he used linguistic markers to tie the story together cohesively. Although Adam showed virtually no lapses in cohesion under narrative speaking conditions, in conversation, his sample was marked by several instances of exophoric and anaphoric reference as well as several instances of nonspecific vocabulary. These differences in use of cohesive devices across speaking tasks suggests that Adam is capable of using more formal, literate style communication. However, his cohesive lapses in conversation could make him difficult to understand in interpersonal communication.
Parent, teacher, and client interviews	See Background Information about Adam in this *Instructor's Supplement* or in the Interview Outcomes in the *CaseFiles* computer program.

[a] 80% confidence interval

[b] Some instructors may take issue with viewing this task as representing the Higher-Order Level. Such differences of perspective and opinion offer rich opportunities for discussion to facilitate critical thinking about appraisal plan specifications and task selection.

INTERPRETATION	Adam's comprehension and production of semantics were within normal limits for his age. His ability to understand and use syntax was below expectations for his age. In addition, Adam's comprehension and production of transitional- and higher-order language structures was enhanced when he drew on his semantic comprehension abilities and reduced when syntactic structures interfered.

(continued)

Appraisal Outcomes: Child-Based Domain—*Continued*

SPEECH

RESULTS

Informal observation

- Voice characteristics   Within normal limits

- Fluency   Within normal limits
  characteristics

Parent, teacher, and   See Background Information about Adam in this *Instructor's Supplement* or in the Interview
client interviews   Outcomes in the *CaseFiles* computer program.

INTERPRETATION   Adam's speech functions appeared adequate to support communication functions.

EXTRALINGUISTIC VARIABLES

RESULTS

Informal observation   Adam was cooperative, and he appeared attentive and motivated during the entire appraisal
session.

	Raw Score	Standard Score	SEM [a]	Percentile Rank
CELF–R (mean standard score = 10, sd = 3) • Oral Directions subtest [b]	21	11	2	63

Parent and teacher   See Background Information about Adam in this *Instructor's Supplement* or in the Interview
interviews   Outcomes in the CaseFiles computer program.

[a] 80% confidence interval

[b] Results of this subtest were interpreted with respect to memory for semantically meaningful but syntactically unrelated material.

INTERPRETATION   Throughout the appraisal, Adam was pleasant, cooperative, and polite. Although it was reported
that Adam often has difficulty concentrating, he attended well throughout the appraisal session and
only occasionally showed signs of fatigue and boredom.

APPRAISAL OUTCOMES: SETTING-BASED DOMAIN

COGNITION

RESULTS

Classroom observation   See School Visit Report in the *CaseFiles* text for findings.

Curricular analysis

- Text: Farah, M., and Karls, A.B. (1990). *The human experience: A world history.* Columbus, OH: Merrill.

- One full chapter from the text was reviewed and the following questions were addressed:

① What basic concepts are presented (e.g., time, space, quantity, quality)?

① Adam's Western Civilization text presents several basic concepts. Time concepts are noted in the reporting of sequential historical events; space concepts are noted in discussions of geographic space and direction; and quality concepts are noted in the use of words such as *strength, power,* and *prosperity.*

② What key mental operations are required (e.g., classification, seriation, number, conservation, temporal ordering, etc.)?

② Analysis of Adam's Western Civilization text indicated a number of mental operations, most notably classification and temporal ordering. With respect to classification, the text demands the ability to work with class inclusion (e.g., empires, dynasties) as well as historical concepts such as major factors that contributed to the fall of the Egyptian empire. With respect to temporal ordering, as a history text, the curriculum relies heavily on historical time and dates.

③ What key thinking skills are required (e.g., causality, inferential thinking, inductive/deductive reasoning)?

③ Adam's Western Civilization text requires several types of thinking skills. Although the narrative itself tends to address relationships explicitly, the Chapter Review demands use of causality, inductive and deductive reasoning, and inferences.

Parent, teacher, and client interviews   See Background Information about Adam in this *Instructor's Supplement* or in the Interview Outcomes in the *CaseFiles* computer program.

INTERPRETATION   The cognitive demands identified in Adam's Western Civilization text appear appropriate for normally developing high school-age students. In addition, most of these cognitive demands are well within the bounds of Adam's abilities. However, given Adam's relative difficulty in making inferences (see Child-Based Language Outcomes), the demands for inferential reasoning may pose some challenges for Adam.

(continued)

LANGUAGE

RESULTS

Classroom observation See School Visit Report in the *CaseFiles* text for findings.

Curricular analysis

- Text: Farah, M., and Karls, A.B. (1990). *The human experience: A world history.* Columbus, OH: Merrill.

- Qualitative analysis of language demands focused on the following linguistic aspects:

  ① Semantic features, including ambiguous words and statements, multiple meaning words, and figurative language

  ① Analysis of the text revealed several instances of ambiguous words (e.g., *under him*, *shook the order of Egyptian life*, *cost them their power*), multiple meaning words (e.g., *drove out*, *strong rulers*), and figurative language (e.g., *more equal contest* invoked a sports metaphor). In addition, some aspects of the text's vocabulary were distracting. For example, because the chapter addressed ancient Egypt, many of the words in the text were foreign. The authors dealt with this element of unfamiliarity in several ways. The pronunciation of the word was indicated in parentheses immediately following its initial appears (e.g., Hyksos [HIHK sohs]), and a definition of the word was embedded in the sentence in which it was first used. In subsequent sentences the word was used frequently and repetitively to reinforce the semantic content.

  ② Sentence structure features, including sentence complexity (e.g., sentence types, complexity, and length) and morphological complexity (e.g., tense, active/passive voice)

  ② A 50-sentence segment from Chapter 1 was analyzed for structural complexity. Sentences in this sample were almost exclusively declarative types, and they averaged 17 words per sentence. Analysis of complexity indicated that approximately 45% of the sentences in the sample were complex or compound-complex. The structural embedding reflected in the length and complexity of the sentences indicated extensive idea compression within the text. From a morphological perspective, simple, active voice, and past tense were reflected in most of the sentences. However, 16% of the 50-sentence sample were written in passive voice.

- Quantitative analysis focused on reading difficulty, or readability

  ① Fry's (1968) strategy for estimating readability

	First 100 Words	Second 100 Words	Third 100 Words	Average
Syllables	144	157	161	154
Sentences	6.5	5.75	7.0	6.41

(continued)

When plotted on Fry's graph for estimating readability, these values suggested that the text was approximately equivalent to a ninth-grade reading level.

② *Flesch Readability Test* (1951)

Average Words Per Sentence	Reading Ease Value
17	59.296

The reading ease score range for "fairly difficult" reading material and 10th- to 12th-grade reading level equivalent is 50 to 60, whereas the range for "standard" difficulty and 8th- and 9th-grade level equivalents is 60 to 70.

Parent, teacher, and client interviews

See Background Information about Adam in this *Instructor's Supplement* or in the Interview Outcomes in the *CaseFiles* computer program.

INTERPRETATION

Differences between the Fry and Flesch analysis notwithstanding, analysis of the language demands inherent in one of Adam's textbooks indicated acceptable semantic and structural complexity for a high school level text and a difficulty level that was approximately equivalent to Adam's grade level. In terms of readability, standard writing averages 17 words per sentence and 147 syllables per 100 words, with reading ease values between 60 and 70 (Flesch, 1951). Analysis of the selection from Adam's text suggested values close to these averages. Moreover, semantic, morphological, and syntactic demands should pose few difficulties for normally achieving high school freshmen. However, Adam demonstrated 30% silent reading comprehension of seventh and eighth grade reading passages and a seventh grade instructional reading level (see HDC Reading Evaluation results in the *CaseFiles* text). In addition, Adam demonstrated difficulties comprehending syntax under both listening and reading condition (see Language Appraisal outcomes above). It is likely that Adam's Western Civilization text places demands on him that are beyond his language abilities. This conclusion is supported by information derived from various interviews.

SUGGESTED DISCUSSION ISSUES

Does Adam demonstrate a language disorder?

Although it is clear that Adam is experiencing difficulty in school, the contribution of language issues to his learning problems needs to be addressed. In that regard, several issues should be highlighted in debriefing discussions with students. First, given Adam's test performances and scores, it is unlikely that he would qualify for services in a public school setting; his difficulties are not severe enough. This issue of documented difficulty versus eligibility is one that clinicians wrestle with regularly, and can be addressed through discussion of definitions of language disorder.

Second, in addressing the status of Adam's language abilities, students' attention should be drawn to patterns in his performances. In that regard, and with respect to levels of language, it is clear that Adam's performances deteriorate as task demands increase: his higher-order level performances are substantially poorer than his performances at basic and transitional levels. Given such a pattern, it is likely that Adam will continue to experience learning difficulties as the language demands of schooling increase.

Third, with respect to areas of language, Adam's semantic skills are clearly superior to his syntactic abilities. This conclusion is supported particularly by his performances on the Listening/Vocabulary and Reading/Vocabulary versus Listening/Grammar and Reading/Grammar subtests from the *TOAL–2*. It is sensible that his difficulties in teasing out meaning variations in surface as opposed to deep structure would interfere with his comprehension. Although he

apparently uses his stronger semantic base to determine meanings, as the language demands in academic settings increase and become more complex and decontextualized, even his relatively strong semantic skills may be overburdened.

Results from appraisals done by examiners from the major study areas of Reading and Special Education through the Human Development Center support these conclusions, and students should be encouraged to use those data to understand Adam's difficulties. Appraisal results from the Reading area deny a broad-based reading disability, although he clearly has some difficulty with comprehension. Similarly, results from the Special Education area also deny a general learning disability, although reading comprehension performances are poorer than performances in other areas.

To what extent do Adam's cognitive and language skills help him meet the demands of his environment?

Although appraisal under the child-based domain provides an understanding of Adam's skills and abilities, Adam's case highlights the importance of addressing setting-based variables in assessment of children with suspected language disorders. In that regard, students should be encouraged to examine the academic areas in which Adam experiences the greatest problems. The curricular analysis information provided in the case study is particularly important here. Adam's difficulties are already in evidence in classes that require extensive language-based, higher-order function: English, Western Civilization, and physical science. Although Adam does not demonstrate a reading disability per se, it is likely that his language skills interfere with his ability to meet the language demands of his current curriculum.

The curricular analysis of Adam's Western Civilization text indicated semantic demands that are within the scope of Adam's abilities. However, cognitive and syntactic demands may pose problems for him. With respect to cognition, the text demands inferential thinking skills, but, as noted on the Making Inferences subtest of the *Test of Language Competence,* Adam demonstrated some difficulty in that area. With respect to syntax, the text demands understanding of passive voice, and it contains a large proportion of complex and compound-complex sentences. Given Adam's relative difficulties in working with various sentence structures, it is likely that the level of syntactic demand inherent in his Western Civilization text will pose problems for his comprehension. In addition, the reading difficulty level of the text, although approximately at Adam's grade level, is at odds with his instructional reading level and his silent reading comprehension skills. This discrepancy suggests that the language demands of his Western Civilization curriculum may pose extreme challenges for Adam's abilities.

This discussion point is not intended to address causality with respect to Adam's academic difficulties. Rather, the intention is to highlight the extent to which Adam's observed skills and abilities will allow him to meet the cognitive and language demands placed on him in important daily settings. In that regard, it is easy to see some of the language-related contributors to Adam's academic problems, even in the absence of a broad-based reading disability.

What predictions can be made about Adam's future language learning and use?

Although Adam's language skills are grossly within normal limits, it is likely that he will continue to experience difficulties in school as the language demands placed on him increase. This conclusion is based on the observation of Adam's relatively poorer skills at the higher-order language level. Debriefing discussions with students might address the predictions they would make as well as the basis for those predictions. Such discussions offer rich opportunities for facilitating students' critical thinking about interpretations of observed assessment performances.

What recommendations should be made for Adam?

Here, again, the issue of demonstrated difficulty versus eligibility should be addressed. Adam represents the kind of student that clinicians who work in the schools may see frequently. Given the likelihood that he would not qualify for services, student clinicians should be encouraged to consider alternative suggestions for helping Adam deal with the language demands of schooling. Such suggestions might involve specific activities for Adam as well as assistance for his teachers in adapting the cognitive and language demands to his ability levels.

Students such as Adam may also seek private services, where issues of eligibility are less relevant. Accordingly, student clinicians should be encouraged to think of intervention targets and strategies for helping Adam work with variations in English syntax.

In making recommendations with Adam, student clinicians should also be encouraged to consider the affective domain. Adam is apparently concerned about his intellectual status. Recommendations should focus on helping him understand the nature of his difficulties and on helping him deal with others who give him a hard time about his academic achievement.

What is the relationship between language and cognition?

Adam's case offers the opportunity to consider the theoretical issue reflected in this question as well as theory-to-practice interpretations associated with it. The position taken in *CaseFiles* is that cognition and language are interrelated and, therefore, assessments of suspected language disorders should address both cognitive and linguistic skills. Some clinicians may disagree with this position, and such disagreement is clearly theoretically grounded. Debriefing discussions that address this issue will help students define and clarify their beliefs about the relationship between language and cognition.

Cognitive tasks used in the actual appraisal as well as Adam's performances on cognitive and language tasks also provide opportunities to consider how these areas relate to each other on both theoretical and theory-to-practice levels. In terms of theory, consider, for example, the *WJPEB–R (Woodcock-Johnson Psycho-Educational Battery–Revised)* cognition tasks and their relationship to language skills. The Concept Formation subtest of the *WJPEB–R* is conceptualized as a measure of rule identification ability, whereas the Analysis-Synthesis subtest is seen as a measure of ability to identify missing pieces of a puzzle. Both of these skills might be viewed as important to language functioning, but it is unclear to which aspects of language these tasks link. Is rule identification associated with syntax and puzzle solution associated with semantics? Or vice versa? Or are both related to only one language area? Perhaps semantics?

From a theory-to-practice perspective, at issue here is whether and in what ways Adam's performances on the *WJPEB–R* predict his linguistic strengths and weaknesses. In that regard, Adam performed within normal limits on both *WJPEB–R* subtests, although his performance was relatively stronger on Concept Formation than on Analysis-Synthesis. Moreover, in terms of language, his strengths were in semantics rather than in syntax. Debriefing discussions might focus on how Adam's observed language performances relate to his performances on the *WJPEB–R* subtests. In addition to this theory-to-practice issue, discussion might also focus on facilitating students' critical thinking about construct validity of tests and how well a given task meshes with what a clinician wants to measure.

What is the relationship between oral and written language?

This question offers students numerous discussion options. Students should be encouraged to consider the question of the relationship between oral and written language per se. In that regard, work by Westby (1991) can be particularly useful in helping students link theory and practice.

Beyond the basic issue of the relationship between oral and written language, this question offers students the opportunity to consider the speech-language pathologist's role in working with students who demonstrate difficulties dealing with written language. Although the HDC reports from Reading and Special Education include general recommendations for improving written language, these recommendations do not provide specific direction for helping Adam derive meaning from print. (See pages 248–255 in the *CaseFiles* text.) At issue is whether and to what extent speech-language pathologists can offer specific assistance to Adam. This point can trigger discussion of the speech-language pathologist's role in working with written language difficulties. Such discussion can focus on the theoretical level to explore students' beliefs about the issue as well as empirical support for their beliefs. On a practical level, discussion can focus on what clinicians can do if their theoretical position supports working with written language problems.

Adam's performances also provide a productive context for considering this relationship on both theoretical and theory-to-practice levels. Narrative construction ability has been found to account for large amounts of variance in reading comprehension across groups defined by reading ability (Jax, 1989). At the macro level of story grammar structure, strong narrative skills are thought to be associated with good reading comprehension whereas weak narrative skills are thought to be associated with poor reading comprehension. Adam's story grammar structure in narrative was relatively weak, supporting his history of reading problems. However, compared to Loban's (1976) data, Adam's structural complexity at the micro level of sentence structure in narrative is commensurate with performances of good readers in his grade. This is at odds with reports of Adam's poor reading skills. At issue here is whether there are contradictions between theoretical grounds and appraisal outcomes for this boy. This issue can be addressed in debriefing discussions designed to help students consider the theoretical relationship between oral and written language, particularly in the face of Adam's performances and history.

In what ways is the planning framework different at various language levels?

As was true with Lisa, visual inspection of the appraisal plan for Adam shows that the decision trees are structured differently at the basic, transitional, and higher-order levels of language. While not unique to Adam, discussion may need to revisit the issue of how language works at different levels of demand.

What differences were noted in students' interview and appraisal plans and those actually implemented in the assessment of Adam?

Students' plans may differ from those actually used in the assessment of Adam. For example, Larson and McKinley (1987, 1995) suggest using a case history form designed specifically for adolescents, as well as a learning style questionnaire. Using these materials with Adam would provide a broader view of his needs than was obtained from the procedures actually used in the assessment. In terms of appraisal, students may have selected different techniques and methods than those actually used with Adam. Debriefing on these differences can help students see that there are numerous ways of approaching assessment of children with suspected language disorders.

References

Bliatout, B.T., Downing, B.T., Lewis, J., and Yang, D. (1988). *Handbook for teaching Hmong-speaking students*. Folsom, CA: Folsom Cordova Unified School District, Southeast Asia Community Resource Center.

Cirrin, F.M. (1994). Assessing language in the classroom and the curriculum. In J.B. Tomblin, H.L. Morris, and D.C. Spriestersbach (Eds.), *Diagnosis in speech-language pathology* (pp. 135–164). San Diego, CA: Singular.

Collier, V.P., and Thomas, W.P. (1989). How quickly can immigrants become proficient in school English? *Journal of Educational Issues of Language Minority Students, 5,* 26–38.

Cummins, J. (1981). The role of primary language development in promoting educational success for language minority students. In California State Department of Education, *Schooling and language minority students: A theoretical framework* (pp. 3–49). Los Angeles, CA: CSULA, EDAC.

Cummins, J. (1984). Wanted: A theoretical framework for relating language proficiency to academic achievement among bilingual students. In C. Rivera (Ed.), *Language proficiency and academic achievement* (pp. 2–19). Clevedon, England: Multilingual Matters.

Damico, J.S. (1991). Descriptive assessment of communicative ability in limited English proficient students. In E.V. Hamayan and J.S. Damico (Eds.), *Limiting bias in the assessment of bilingual students* (pp. 157–217). Austin, TX: Pro-Ed.

Gruenewald, L., and Pollak, S. (1990). *Language interaction in curriculum and instruction* (2nd ed.). Austin, TX: Pro-Ed.

Jax, V.A. (1989). Narrative construction by children learning English as a second language: A precursor to reading comprehension (Doctoral dissertation, University of California, Los Angeles, 1988). *Dissertation Abstracts International, 49,* 2133A.

Johns, K.M. (1988). *How children learn a second language*. Bloomington, IN: Phi Delta Kappa Educational Foundation.

Loban, W. (1976). *Language development: Kindergarten through grade twelve.* Urbana, IL: National Council of Teachers of English.

Larson, V. Lord, and McKinley, N.L. (1987). *Communication assessment and intervention strategies for adolescents.* Eau Claire, WI: Thinking Publications.

Larson, V. Lord, and McKinley, N.L. (1995). *Language disorders in older students: Preadolescents and adolescents.* Eau Claire, WI: Thinking Publications.

McInnis, K.M., Petracchi, H.E., and Morgenbesser, M. (1990). *The Hmong in America: Providing ethnic-sensitive health, education, and human services.* Dubuque, IA: Kendall/Hunt.

Saville-Troike, M. (1987). Private speech: Second language learning during the "silent" period. *Papers and Reports on Child Language, 26,* 104–115.Wasserman, S. (1993). *Getting down to cases.* New York: Teachers College Press.

Welty, W.M. (July/August, 1989). Discussion method teaching: How to make it work. *Change, 41–49.*

Westby, C.E. (1991). Learning to talk—talking to learn: Oral-literate language differences. In C.S. Simon (Ed.), *Communication skills and classroom success: Assessment and therapy methodologies for language-learning disabled students* (pp. 334–355). Eau Claire, WI: Thinking Publications.

Note: References for appraisal instruments and procedures cited in this *Instructor's Supplement* are available in Appendix A of the *CaseFiles* text.